THE Saint's Plate

BY EMILY FRISELLA

ISBN 13: 978-1-63489-234-6

Library of Congress Catalog Number: 2019939099

Printed in the United States.

First Printing: 2019

Cover and interior design by Emily Shaffer Rodvold at Lift Creative.

Published by Wise Ink Creative Publishing.

Wise Ink Creative Publishing

807 Broadway St. NE, Suite 46

Minneapolis, MN 55413

wiseink.com

Contents

Living a healthy lifestyle is a passion of mine. That includes overall wellness, fitness, and maintaining a healthy diet. With this book, it is my hope that you will find or continue your love of treating your body well with good-for-you recipes that are easy to create and easy to track by using the nutrition information provided.

You will find recipes that will please your palate as well as your waistline—all without breaking the bank or having to search high and low for exotic ingredients. I want you to feel confident in the kitchen to provide truly healthy, made-from-scratch recipes for yourself and your family and realize that "diet food" doesn't have to taste like cardboard and broken dreams.

I can't wait for you to dive into the pages and find some new favorite recipes to create and enjoy while keeping your goals and progress on the right track.

–Emily Frisella

Vegetarian Lasagna

12 whole wheat or gluten-free lasagna noodles, cooked
2 tablespoons olive oil
1 cup red bell pepper, chopped
2 cups zucchini, sliced and quartered
1 cup squash, sliced and quartered
5 cloves fresh garlic, minced
3 cups mushrooms, sliced
6 ounces baby spinach
3 tablespoons fresh basil, chopped
15-ounce container of light ricotta cheese
⅓ cup parmesan cheese, grated
1 teaspoon salt
½ teaspoon pepper
1 egg, beaten
2 cups low-fat mozzarella cheese, shredded
2 cups canned tomato basil sauce (I used Del Monte brand)

Preheat oven to 375°.

Boil and cook lasagna noodles. While noodles cook, prepare the following:

In a large skillet, heat 1 tablespoon of the olive oil over medium to high heat. Add in bell pepper, zucchini, squash, and half the minced garlic. Stir and cook for 5–6 minutes, then transfer to a bowl.

Next, heat the remaining 1 tablespoon of olive oil and add in the mushroom and remaining garlic. Cook for 4–5 minutes, then add in spinach. Cook until spinach wilts. Transfer mixture to a different bowl, then stir in the chopped basil.

In a small bowl, combine the ricotta cheese, parmesan cheese, salt, pepper, and egg.

To layer the lasagna: Add 4 tablespoons of the canned sauce to the bottom of a 9-by-9 inch pan. Then top with 1 layer of noodles, trimming off any excess. Spoon half the spinach-mushroom mixture on top of the noodles, then top with half the ricotta mixture. Add another layer of noodles, then half the remaining tomato sauce, then all the zucchini mixture, and then 1 cup of mozzarella cheese. Add a layer of noodles and top with the remaining spinach-mushroom mix, then the remaining ricotta cheese mixture. Top with a layer of the remaining noodles and spread the remaining tomato basil sauce over the top. Finally, add the remaining mozzarella cheese, place in the oven, and bake for 45 minutes.

MAKES 9 SERVINGS
Serving size: one 3-by-3-inch square
Calories: 283
Fat: 11g
Saturated fat: 5g
Polyunsaturated fat: 1g
Monounsaturated fat: 2g
Trans fat: 0g
Cholesterol: 52mg
Sodium: 716mg
Carbohydrates: 29g
Fiber: 5g
Sugar: 7g
Protein: 20g
Iron: 11g
Potassium: 441mg

Bacon Chicken Zoodle Bowl

1 tablespoon butter
5 cups zucchini noodles ("zoodles")
1 clove minced garlic
8 ounces sliced grilled chicken
2 strips precooked center-cut bacon
1 tablespoon fresh basil, chopped
¼ cup cherry tomatoes, sliced into quarters
salt and pepper to taste
1 tablespoon parmesan cheese shreds
⅛ cup low-fat mozzarella cheese

Using a nonstick pan, melt butter over medium heat.

Add your zoodles and minced garlic to the pan. Toss to combine and cook 2–3 minutes.

Next, add your chicken, bacon, basil, and cherry tomatoes, and sprinkle with salt and pepper to taste. Toss to combine. Continue to cook until zoodles are tender.

Finally, plate your dish and sprinkle with the parmesan cheese shreds and mozzarella.

MAKES 2 ZOODLE BOWLS
Serving size: half of recipe
Calories: 487
Fat: 14g
Saturated fat: 6g
Polyunsaturated fat: 0g
Monounsaturated fat: 0g
Trans fat: 0g
Cholesterol: 31
Sodium: 313
Carbohydrates: 11g
Fiber: 5.5g
Sugar: 5.5g
Protein: 36g
Iron: 0.5g
Potassium: 1354mg

Asian Chicken Wrap with Peanut Sauce

WRAP

3 ounces marinated garlic soy grilled chicken
⅓ cup red cabbage, shredded
⅓ cup green cabbage, shredded
⅛ cup carrot
1 tablespoon peanuts
1 tablespoon green onions, green and light green portion only
½ tablespoon cilantro
1 whole wheat wrap

PEANUT SAUCE

can be made in a larger batch ahead of time

2 tablespoons creamy peanut
1 tablespoon rice vinegar
½ teaspoon fresh grated gingerroot
½ tablespoon low sodium soy sauce
pinch of fresh garlic
dash of cayenne pepper

CHICKEN

1 boneless, skinless chicken breast, tenderized to even thickness
1 teaspoon olive oil
¼ teaspoon dried oregano
1 teaspoon soy sauce
½ teaspoon fresh garlic clove, peeled and minced finely
½ teaspoon salt
⅛ teaspoon cayenne pepper
dash of black pepper
nonstick cooking spray

Pat chicken breast dry and place into large Ziploc bag.

In a medium bowl combine the olive oil, oregano, soy sauce, garlic, salt, cayenne, and black pepper. Pour mixture into the plastic bag with the chicken.

Seal the bag and gently shake to coat the chicken. Place in fridge and let it marinade for an hour.

Heat skillet or grill pan, and grill chicken for 5 minutes per side or until juices run clear. Remove from pan and let rest 10 minutes, then slice into thin strips.

Combine chicken, red and green cabbage, carrot shreds, peanuts, green onions, and cilantro in a bowl, mix in peanut sauce to coat, and roll everything up in the whole wheat wrap.

MAKES 1 WRAP
Serving size: 1 wrap
Calories: 502
Fat: 22g
Saturated fat: 4g
Polyunsaturated fat: 0g
Monounsaturated fat: 0g
Trans fat: 1g
Cholesterol: 65mg
Sodium: 976mg
Carbohydrates: 41g
Fiber: 7g
Sugar: 12g
Protein: 40g
Iron: 4g

Grilled Chicken Power Bowl

4 ounces garlic soy marinated grilled chicken breast

½ cup cooked brown rice

1 cup steamed broccoli

2 tablespoon low-sodium soy sauce served on side

CHICKEN

1 boneless, skinless chicken breast, tenderized to even thickness

1 teaspoon olive oil

¼ teaspoon dried oregano

1 teaspoon soy sauce

½ teaspoon fresh garlic clove, peeled and minced finely

½ teaspoon salt

⅛ teaspoon cayenne pepper

dash of black pepper

nonstick cooking spray

Pat chicken breast dry and place into large Ziploc bag.

In a medium bowl combine the olive oil, oregano, soy sauce, garlic, salt, cayenne, and black pepper. Pour mixture into the plastic bag with the chicken.

Seal the bag and gently shake to coat the chicken. Place in fridge and let it marinade for an hour.

Heat skillet or grill pan, and grill chicken for 5 minutes per side or until juices run clear. Remove from pan and let rest 10 minutes, then slice into thin strips.

Put rice in center of bowl and top with chicken and broccoli. Pour soy sauce on top. (This recipe is very easy to prep ahead of time!)

.

MAKES 1 BOWL
Serving size: 1 bowl
Calories: 313
Fat: 4g
Saturated fat: 0g
Trans fat: 0g
Cholesterol: 70mg
Sodium: 1130mg
Carbohydrates: 31g
Fiber: 5g
Sugar: 4g
Protein: 33g
Iron: 3g

Lemon Blueberry Protein Doughnut

DOUGHNUT

nonstick cooking spray
⅓ cup coconut flour
⅓ cup Truvia or Stevia
⅓ cup 1stPhorm Level-1 Vanilla Ice Cream protein powder
¼ teaspoon salt
1 teaspoon baking powder
⅓ cup & 2 tablespoons unsweetened almond or coconut milk
1 teaspoon lemon extract
2 tablespoons unsweetened applesauce
2 egg whites
1 whole egg
⅔ cup fresh or frozen blueberries

GLAZE

Zest of 1 lemon (optional)
2 tablespoons coconut oil
3 – 4 tablespoons 1stPhorm Level-1 Vanilla Ice Cream Protein Powder

Preheat oven to 325°.

Spray 6-count doughnut pan with nonstick cooking spray until well covered.

In a small bowl, combine flour, Truvia, protein powder, salt, and baking powder.

In a medium bowl, combine milk, lemon extract, applesauce, egg whites, and egg.

Next, in a small bowl, add the blueberries and just enough of the dry ingredient mixture to coat the blueberries. (This keeps them from sinking to the bottom.)

Pour your dry ingredients into the wet ingredients and whisk until well combined. Then gently fold in the blueberries and spoon into the doughnut pan to the top of each doughnut mold.

Bake for 18–20 minutes or until a toothpick comes out clean. Remove from oven and allow to cool 3–5 minutes, then turn doughnuts out onto cooling rack. Once fully cool, you may glaze them.

For Glaze:

In a small microwavable bowl, microwave the coconut oil until just melted. Stir in 3 tablespoons of protein, adding 1 additional tablespoon if needed to achieve a thin, yogurt-like consistency. Add the fresh zest of 1 lemon if you would like more lemon flavor in the icing.

Turn doughnuts over and dip into glaze. Return to cooling rack, then place glazed doughnuts in fridge for 10–15 minutes until set. Store in airtight container in the fridge or on the countertop. These freeze great too!

MAKES 6 DOUGHNUTS
Serving size: 1 doughnut
Calories: 143
Fat: 7g
Saturated fat: 5.5g
Trans fat: 0g
Cholesterol: 47mg
Sodium: 203mg
Carbohydrates: 7g
Fiber: 3g
Sugar: 3g
Protein: 10g
Iron: 5.5g

Unwrapped Breakfast Burrito

- nonstick cooking spray
- 4 eggs
- 4 egg whites
- ¼ cup unsweetened almond milk
- ¼ teaspoon salt
- ¼ teaspoon black pepper
- ½ cup low-fat shredded cheddar cheese
- 1 cup fresh baby spinach, chopped
- 6 low-fat bacon slices, precooked
- 2 green onions, green and light green portion only, chopped
- ¼ cup chopped mushrooms
- ¼ cup diced tomatoes

Preheat oven to 350°.

In a medium bowl, combine eggs and egg whites. Whisk until beaten. Add in remaining ingredients and mix well.

Spray a muffin tin well with nonstick cooking spray in 9 of the cavities. Fill ¾ full with egg mixture. Bake for 20–25 minutes or until toothpick comes out clean.

Remove from oven and allow to cool 20 minutes before removing from the tin. When it's time to remove, carefully run a butter knife around the edges to easily lift the egg from the tin.

Store in an airtight container in the fridge and heat in microwave for 45 seconds to 1 minute when you are ready to enjoy.

*These freeze wonderfully, so feel free to make in larger batches for a delicious grab-and-go breakfast!

MAKES 9
Serving size: 1 muffin
Calories: 90
Fat: 5g
Saturated fat: 1g
Polyunsaturated fat: 0g
Monounsaturated fat: 0.5g
Trans fat: 0g
Cholesterol: 87mg
Sodium: 178mg
Carbohydrates: 1g
Fiber: 0 g
Sugar: 0g
Protein: 9g
Iron: 3g

Clean & Lean Breakfast Sandwich

3 egg whites
¼ cup chopped spinach
2 slices turkey bacon
1 tomato slice
1 thin slice cheddar cheese
salt to taste
pepper to taste
1 whole wheat English muffin, toasted

Add egg whites and spinach to a nonstick pan and cook until eggs are scrambled. While egg whites cook, toast English muffin.

Place all ingredients on English muffin and serve.

MAKES 1 SANDWICH
Serving size: 1 sandwich
Calories: 291
Fat: 10g
Saturated fat: 2g
Trans fat: 0g
Cholesterol: 30mg
Sodium: 672mg
Carbohydrates: 26g
Fiber: 3g
Sugar: 2g
Protein: 24g
Iron: 3g

Cranberry Oat Protein Cookies

- ½ cup old-fashioned oatmeal
- 3 scoops 1stPhorm Level-1 Cinnamon Cookie Batter protein powder
- 1 cup unsweetened applesauce
- 2 ripe bananas, mashed
- ¼ cup chopped walnuts
- ⅓ cup reduced-sugar dried cranberries
- 1 teaspoon vanilla extract
- 1 teaspoon ground cinnamon

Preheat oven to 350°.

Line 2 baking sheets with parchment paper.

In a medium bowl, combine all ingredients and stir by hand until well mixed. Allow to rest for 10 minutes. (This helps the oatmeal absorb some liquid.)

Using a medium cookie scoop or a tablespoon, drop batter onto parchment-lined baking sheets, allowing 2 inches between cookies.

Place cookies in the oven and bake for 14–17 minutes or until bottoms are light golden brown. Remove from oven and allow the cookies to rest on the baking sheet for 2–3 minutes, then transfer to cooling rack. Allow cookies to cool completely and store in an airtight container.

MAKES 28 COOKIES
Serving size: 1 cookie
Calories: 48
Fat: 11g
Saturated fat: 0
Trans fat: 0g
Cholesterol: 6mg
Sodium: 13mg
Carbohydrates: 7g
Fiber: 1g
Sugar: 2g
Protein: 3.5g
Iron: 1g

Garlic Lemon Roasted Chicken

2 boneless, skinless chicken breasts
nonstick cooking spray
1 teaspoon lemon zest
2 teaspoons lemon juice
2 teaspoons olive oil
1 teaspoon minced garlic
½ teaspoon dried oregano
¼ teaspoon salt
¼ teaspoon pepper

Preheat oven to 400°.

Pound chicken breast to approximately ½-inch thickness.

Place chicken on a baking sheet sprayed with nonstick cooking spray.

In a small bowl, combine remaining ingredients.

Carefully brush on the seasoning blend and bake for 20–22 minutes or until chicken juices run clear.

MAKES 2 SERVINGS
Serving size: 4 ounces
Calories: 174
Fat: 6g
Saturated fat: 1g
Polyunsaturated fat: 0g
Monounsaturated fat: 3g
Trans fat: 0g
Cholesterol: 65mg
Sodium: 371mg
Carbohydrates: 1g
Fiber: 0g
Sugar: 0g
Protein: 26g
Iron: 5mg
Potassium: 14g

Snickerdoodle Protein Doughnuts

DOUGHNUTS

nonstick cooking spray
⅓ cup coconut flour
⅓ cup Stevia
⅓ cup 1stPhorm Level-1 Cinnamon Cookie Batter protein powder
1 teaspoon ground cinnamon
¼ teaspoon salt
1 teaspoon baking powder
1 teaspoon vanilla extract
2 tablespoons applesauce
⅓ cup & 2 tablespoons unsweetened vanilla almond milk
2 egg whites
1 whole egg

GLAZE

2 tablespoons coconut oil
½ scoop 1stPhorm Level-1 Cinnamon Cookie Batter protein powder
additional toppings: sprinkles, nuts, or mini chocolate chips

Preheat oven to 325°.

Lightly spray doughnut pan with nonstick cooking spray.

In a small bowl, mix together coconut flour, Stevia, protein powder, cinnamon, salt, and baking powder.

In a medium bowl, mix together remaining doughnut ingredients.

Add the contents of small bowl to medium bowl and mix well.

Spoon into doughnut pan and bake for 20–23 minutes.

While the doughnuts bake, start on the glaze. In a small bowl, but large enough to dip doughnuts in, add 2 tablespoons coconut oil and microwave 15–20 seconds, just enough to soften the oil and begin to melt it. You don't want it completely melted.

Add a small amount of the protein powder at a time and mix until all protein is used.

Once the doughnuts are done, let them rest in pan for 2–3 minutes, then turn them out onto cooling rack. Allow doughnuts to cool completely.

Dip the doughnuts into the glaze and place on a plate or tray. Once all are glazed, place in the fridge and let glaze set 4–5 minutes. Remove and place in an airtight container, and enjoy!

MAKES 6 DOUGHNUTS
Serving size: 1 doughnut
Calories: 139
Fat: 7g
Saturated fat: 5.5g
Polyunsaturated fat: 0g
Monounsaturated fat: 0g
Trans fat: 0g
Cholesterol: 47mg
Sodium: 199mg
Carbohydrates: 6.5g
Fiber: 3g
Sugar: 1.5g
Protein: 10g
Iron: 5.5g
Potassium: 49mg

Peanut Butter Protein Cookies

½ cup creamy peanut butter
½ cup Splenda or Stevia
⅓ cup 1stPhorm Level-1 Chocolate Peanut Butter Cup protein powder
3 tablespoons liquid egg whites or 1 large egg white
1 teaspoon baking soda
nonstick cooking spray

Preheat oven to 350°.

In a medium bowl, mix together peanut butter, Splenda, and protein powder.

In a small bowl, combine egg whites and baking soda.

Add egg white mixture to peanut butter mixture and mix until smooth. Drop mixture onto parchment-lined baking sheet, forming 12 cookies.

Lightly spray the back of a fork with nonstick cooking spray, and press vertically and horizontally on top of cookies to achieve the classic peanut butter cookie cross-pattern top.

Bake for 9–11 minutes or until lightly golden brown.

Let cool on baking sheet 2 minutes, then transfer to cooling rack. Allow to cool completely, then store in an airtight container.

MAKES 12 COOKIES
Serving size: 1 cookie
Calories: 79
Fat: 5.5g
Saturated fat: 1g
Polyunsaturated fat: 0g
Monounsaturated fat: 1g
Trans fat: 0g
Cholesterol: 5mg
Sodium: 172mg
Carbohydrates: 2g
Fiber: 0.5g
Sugar: 1g
Protein: 5g
Iron: 1g
Potassium: 12.5mg

Lemon Shortbread Protein Cookies

COOKIES

2 scoops 1stPhorm Phormula-1 Lemon Meringue protein powder
1½ cups almond flour
1 teaspoon baking powder
¼ teaspoon salt
¼ cup powdered stevia
⅓ cup finely crushed graham cracker crumbs
½ teaspoon lemon extract
2 tablespoons melted butter
1 egg, lightly beaten
⅛ teaspoon liquid Stevia
4 teaspoons water

COATING (OPTIONAL)

¼ cup white chocolate chip morsels
1 teaspoon lemon extract

Preheat oven to 300°.

In a medium bowl, add protein powder, almond flour, baking powder, salt, powdered Stevia, and graham crackers. Stir to combine.

In a small bowl, add the lemon extract, butter, egg, liquid Stevia, and water. Whisk together, then pour the wet ingredients into the dry ingredients and knead with hands or two spoons until dough is mixed well. Dough will be slightly crumbly. Keep working and pressing together until you can form a semi-solid ball of dough.

Place ball of dough on a piece of parchment paper. Cover with another sheet of parchment and roll with a rolling pin until dough is approximately ¼-inch thick.

Line two baking sheets with parchment paper and, using a cookie cutter (I used a 2-inch circle), cut out cookies and place them on the parchment paper with 1 inch between them. Continue to rework dough, roll flat, and cut cookies out until all dough is used.

Place cookies in oven and bake for 9–11 minutes. Remove from oven and place onto a cooling rack. Cookies will continue to crisp as they cool.

Add white chocolate morsels to a double boiler on the stove or a microwave-safe bowl. Heat until melted, stirring often to keep it smooth and even. Once melted, stir in 1 teaspoon lemon extract.

Once cookies are completely cool, place them on wax paper–lined baking sheet or something that will fit in your fridge. Pour white chocolate and lemon extract mixture into a large plastic Ziploc bag, snip the corner off, and drizzle over the top of the cookies.

Add any additional toppings while chocolate is still wet. Once all cookies are coated, place in the fridge and allow to cool and set for 15–20 minutes or until chocolate hardens. Remove from fridge and place in an airtight container. Store at room temperature.

MAKES 27 TWO-INCH COOKIES
Serving size: 1 cookie (no coating)
Calories: 57
Fat: 4g
Saturated fat: 0.5g
Polyunsaturated fat: 0g
Monounsaturated fat: 0g
Trans fat: 0g
Cholesterol: 9mg
Sodium: 56mg
Carbohydrates: 2g
Fiber: 0.5g
Sugar: 0.5g
Protein: 3g
Iron: 2g
Potassium: 2.5mg

Mint Chocolate Chip Protein Doughnuts

DOUGHNUTS

nonstick cooking spray
⅓ cup coconut flour
⅓ cup Stevia
1 scoop 1stPhorm Level-1 Mint Ice Cream Sandwich protein powder
¼ teaspoon salt
1 teaspoon baking powder
1 teaspoon vanilla extract
2 tablespoons applesauce
⅓ cup & 2 tablespoons unsweetened vanilla almond milk
2 egg whites
1 whole egg

GLAZE

2 tablespoons coconut oil
½ scoop 1stPhorm Level-1 Mint Ice Cream Sandwich protein powder

OPTIONAL

sprinkles, nuts, mini chocolate chips, etc.

Preheat oven to 325°.

Spray doughnut pan with nonstick cooking spray.

In a small bowl mix together coconut flour, Stevia, protein powder, salt, and baking powder.

In a medium bowl mix together vanilla extract, applesauce, almond milk, egg whites, and egg.

Add the small bowl to the medium bowl and mix well.

Spoon into doughnut pan and bake for 20–23 minutes. Once done, let rest in pan 2–3 minutes, then turn doughnuts out onto cooling rack.

While doughnuts cool, make the glaze. Add 2 tablespoons coconut oil to a small bowl, large enough to dip doughnuts in, and microwave 15–20 seconds, just enough to soften the oil and begin to melt it. You don't want it completely melted.

Slowly add protein powder and mix until all protein is used. (Glaze should be a consistency similar to yogurt.)

When doughnuts are completely cool, dip them into the glaze and place on a plate or tray. Once all are glazed, place in the fridge and let glaze set 4–5 minutes. Remove and place in an airtight container. Enjoy!

MAKES 6 DOUGHNUTS
Serving size: 1 doughnut
Calories: 139
Fat: 7g
Saturated fat: 5.5g
Polyunsaturated fat: 0g
Monounsaturated fat: 0g
Trans fat: 0g
Cholesterol: 47mg
Sodium: 199mg
Carbohydrates: 6.5g
Protein: 10g
Fiber: 3g
Sugar: 1.5g
Potassium: 4g
Iron: 5.5g

Lemon Blueberry Smoothie

- 1 cup frozen blueberries
- 1 cup unsweetened almond milk
- 1 Scoop 1stPhorm Level-1 Vanilla Ice Cream protein powder
- 1 teaspoon lemon zest
- 1 teaspoon lemon juice
- 1 teaspoon Truvia or Splenda

Layer all ingredients in a blender from liquid to solid, then blend until smooth and thick.

MAKES 1 SMOOTHIE
Calories: 221
Fat: 6g
Saturated fat: 2g
Polyunsaturated fat: 1g
Monounsaturated fat: 2g
Trans fat: 0g
Cholesterol: 60mg
Sodium: 275mg
Carbohydrates: 9g
Fiber: 2g
Sugar: 5g
Protein: 25g
Iron: 2g
Potassium: 64mg

Just Peachy Smoothie

1 cup unsweetened almond milk
1 cup frozen peaches
1 teaspoon Stevia
1 Scoop 1stPhorm Level-1 Vanilla Ice Cream protein powder

Layer all ingredients in a blender from liquid to solid, then blend until smooth and thick.

MAKES 1 SMOOTHIE
Calories: 249
Fat: 6g
Saturated fat: 2g
Polyunsaturated fat: 0g
Monounsaturated fat: 2g
Trans fat: 0g
Cholesterol: 60mg
Sodium: 275mg
Carbohydrates: 17g
Fiber: 2g
Sugar: 11g
Protein: 26g
Iron: 4g
Potassium: 305mg

Snickerdoodle Protein Balls

¾ cup gluten-free vanilla Chex cereal
½ cup almond flour
½ cup 1stPhorm Level-1 Cinnamon Cookie Batter protein powder
½ tablespoon cinnamon
¼ cup honey
¼ cup creamy almond butter*
1 teaspoon vanilla extract
½ tablespoon water

Place cereal in a plastic bag and crush.

Combine almond flour, protein powder, and cinnamon in a medium bowl.

Next, stir in the honey, almond butter, vanilla extract, and water.

Mix well with your hands or with wooden spoons. Dough will be slightly crumbly.

Press dough into 18 1-inch balls. Place on a wax lined tray or plate, cover, and let chill for 2 hours until cool.

Keep refrigerated until ready to eat.

*You can use peanut butter, but you will have more of a peanut taste. Almond butter has a more muted flavor

MAKES 18 BALLS
Serving size: 1 ball
Calories: 68
Fat: 3.5g
Saturated fat: 0g
Polyunsaturated fat: 0g
Monounsaturated fat: 0g
Trans fat: 0g
Cholesterol: 5mg
Sodium: 32mg
Carbohydrates: 6.5g
Fiber: 0.5g
Sugar: 4.5g
Protein: 3.5g
Iron: 4g
Potassium: 5.5mg

Chocolate-Covered Cherry Smoothie

1 cup frozen cherries
1 cup unsweetened almond milk
1 Scoop 1stPhorm Level-1 Vanilla Milkshake protein powder
1 tablespoon cocoa powder
½ tablespoon dark chocolate chips

Layer all ingredients in a blender from liquid to solid, then blend until smooth and thick.

MAKES 1 SMOOTHIE
Calories: 334
Fat: 8g
Saturated fat: 4g
Polyunsaturated fat: 0g
Monounsaturated fat: 2g
Trans fat: 0g
Cholesterol: 60mg
Sodium: 340mg
Carbohydrates: 33g
Fiber: 6g
Sugar: 23g
Protein: 27g
Iron: 6g
Potassium: 345mg

Island Breeze Smoothie

1 cup frozen pineapple
½ cup unsweetened coconut milk
1 scoop 1stPhorm Level-1 Vanilla Ice Cream protein powder

Layer all ingredients in a blender from liquid to solid, then blend until smooth and thick.

MAKES 1 SMOOTHIE
Calories: 264
Fat: 8g
Saturated fat: 6g
Polyunsaturated fat: 0g
Monounsaturated fat: 0g
Trans fat: 0g
Cholesterol: 60mg
Sodium: 130mg
Carbohydrates: 28g
Fiber: 3g
Sugar: 19g
Protein: 25g
Iron: 6g
Potassium: 255mg

Strawberry Nutella Smoothie

1 cup frozen strawberries
1 scoop 1stPhorm Level-1 Strawberry Milkshake protein powder
1 cup unsweetened almond milk
2 tablespoons Nutella

Layer all ingredients in a blender from liquid to solid, then blend until smooth and thick.

MAKES 1 SMOOTHIE
Calories: 436
Fat: 15g
Saturated fat: 6g
Polyunsaturated fat: 1g
Monounsaturated fat: 2g
Trans fat: 0g
Cholesterol: 60mg
Sodium: 289mg
Carbohydrates: 44g
Fiber: 6g
Sugar: 31g
Protein: 27g
Potassium: 362g
Iron: 15g

Protein Cereal Bars

2 cups gluten-free cereal, such as Barbara's Puffins Cereal, Cheerios, or Chex

1 cup and 2 tablespoons 1stPhorm Level-1 Vanilla Ice Cream 1stPhorm protein powder

½ cup honey

½ cup almond butter

In a medium mixing bowl, combine protein powder and cereal. Gently mix to combine.

In a small microwavable bowl, combine almond butter and honey. Heat for 30–45 seconds until mixture is smooth and creamed together.

Pour almond butter mixture over cereal and fold in with a spatula until evenly combined.

Spoon mixture into loaf pan lined with wax paper and press down batter until evenly distributed. Press firm enough to compact the batter, but not hard enough that you crush the cereal. Place in the freezer for 30 minutes.

Remove and slice into 7 equal bars. Place bars in an airtight container or package individually in sandwich baggies and place in fridge until you're ready to enjoy.

MAKES 7 BARS
Serving size: 1 bar
Calories: 282
Fat: 12g
Saturated fat: 2g
Polyunsaturated fat: 0g
Monounsaturated fat: 0g
Trans fat: 0g
Cholesterol: 25mg
Sodium: 86mg
Carbohydrates: 34g
Fiber: 3g
Sugar: 22g
Protein: 15g
Iron: 5g
Potassium: 37mg

Caramel Peanut Butter Chocolate Chip Cookie

⅔ cup old fashioned oats
1 cup 1stPhorm Level-1 Caramel Latte protein powder
1 teaspoon baking soda
1 cup natural peanut butter
⅔ cup brown sugar substitute
2 eggs
1 ½ teaspoons vanilla extract
½ cup chocolate chips

Preheat oven to 350°.

In a small bowl combine oats, protein, and baking soda.

In a large bowl, blend with hand mixer: peanut butter, brown sugar substitute, eggs, and vanilla extract.

Add the dry ingredients to the wet ingredients and mix using a hand mixer until well combined. Then, using a wooden spoon, fold in the chocolate chips.

Drop on ungreased baking sheet using a medium cookie scoop or tablespoon. Lightly press the top to slightly flatten. Bake for 9–11 minutes, then remove from oven and allow cookies to cool 2–3 minutes.

Remove the cookies from the baking sheet and place onto a cooling rack. Let cool completely, then transfer to an airtight container.

MAKES 2 DOZEN
Serving size: 1 cookie
Calories: 186
Fat: 12g
Saturated fat: 3g
Polyunsaturated fat: 0g
Monounsaturated fat: 0g
Trans fat: 0g
Cholesterol: 24mg
Sodium: 172mg
Carbohydrates: 10g
Fiber: 2g
Sugar: 5g
Protein: 9g
Iron: 4g
Potassium: 6mg

Baked Chicken Parmesan

1 cup panko breadcrumbs
salt and pepper to taste
3 egg whites
4 chicken breasts, tenderized to make chicken even thickness
5 Roma tomatoes, diced
2 garlic cloves, minced
½ teaspoon lemon juice
4 tablespoons fresh basil, chopped
1 teaspoon fresh oregano, chopped
½ cup low-fat mozzarella

Preheat oven to 400°.

In a medium bowl, combine breadcrumbs, salt, and pepper.

In an additional medium bowl, add egg whites.

Line a baking sheet with parchment paper. Dip chicken breasts one at a time into egg white bowl, then place into bowl of breadcrumb mixture and lightly pat so breadcrumbs adhere to chicken. Coat both sides, then place on baking sheet.

Bake chicken for 20 minutes.

While chicken bakes, heat a medium skillet over low-medium heat. Add in tomatoes, minced garlic, lemon juice, and salt and pepper. Allow to simmer 3–4 minutes. Then add in the basil and oregano. Simmer 2–3 minutes, then remove from heat.

When chicken is done baking, remove from oven. Top chicken with the tomato sauce and sprinkle each chicken breast with half the low-fat mozzarella. Return to oven and broil for 2–3 minutes or until mozzarella is melted and lightly browned on top.

MAKES 4 SERVINGS
Serving size: 4 ounces
Calories: 238
Fat: 5g
Saturated fat: 1.5g
Polyunsaturated fat: 0g
Monounsaturated fat: 0g
Trans fat: 0g
Cholesterol: 7mg
Sodium: 161mg
Carbohydrates: 14g
Fiber: 1g
Sugar: 1g
Protein: 28g
Iron: 4g
Potassium: 70mg

Soy Cilantro Chicken

4 chicken breasts, tenderized to make chicken even thickness
salt and pepper to taste
nonstick cooking spray
6 tablespoons low-sodium soy sauce
2 tablespoons fresh cilantro, chopped

Season chicken with salt and pepper on both sides.

Heat a grill pan or skillet over medium heat. Once grill pan is hot, spray with nonstick cooking spray, then lay chicken breasts into pan.

Grill for 3-4 minutes, then drizzle 3 tablespoons soy sauce over one side of the chicken breasts. Sprinkle 1 tablespoon of fresh cilantro over chicken breasts.

Continue to cook for 1–2 minutes, then turn chicken over and cook for 2–3 minutes. Drizzle remaining soy sauce over the chicken, then sprinkle with remaining cilantro.

Allow to cook 1–2 more minutes or until center of chicken has reached 160°. Remove chicken from pan and let it rest 5 minutes before serving.

MAKES 4 SERVINGS
Serving size: 4 ounces
Calories: 217
Fat: 4g
Saturated fat: 0g
Polyunsaturated fat: 0g
Monounsaturated fat: 0g
Trans fat: 0g
Cholesterol: 0mg
Sodium: 690mg
Carbohydrates: 3g
Fiber: 0g
Sugar: 1.5g
Protein: 28g
Iron: 0g
Potassium: 2.5mg

Easy Bruschetta Chicken

- nonstick cooking spray
- 2 boneless, skinless chicken breasts tenderized to make even thickness
- dash of salt to taste
- 2 teaspoons of garlic, minced
- 3 teaspoons Italian seasoning
- ⅓ cup balsamic vinegar
- 1 ½ teaspoons brown sugar
- ¼ cup red onion, diced
- 5 tablespoons of fresh basil
- ½ cup Roma tomatoes, chopped
- ¼ cup fresh parmesan cheese shreds

Season grill pan with nonstick cooking spray and heat over medium heat.

Sprinkle chicken breasts on both sides with salt, garlic, and Italian seasoning. Place seasoned chicken in pan and cook for 5 minutes per side or until internal temperature is 160°, then remove from grill pan, place on a plate, and let rest.

While the chicken is grilling, combine the balsamic vinegar and brown sugar in a saucepan on high heat. Bring to a boil, then allow to simmer 5–7 minutes to cook, until thick.

In a medium bowl, combine red onion, basil, and tomatoes. Scoop onto each chicken breast.

Sprinkle with parmesan cheese, drizzle the balsamic glaze over the top, and serve.

MAKES 2 SERVINGS
Serving size: 4 ounces
Calories: 294
Fat: 7g
Saturated fat: 1.5g
Polyunsaturated fat: 0g
Monounsaturated fat: 1g
Trans fat: 0g
Cholesterol: 7mg
Sodium: 589mg
Carbohydrates: 14g
Fiber: 1g
Sugar: 10g
Protein: 30g
Iron: 7g
Potassium: 204mg

Andy's Chicken

nonstick cooking spray
4 tablespoons oat flour
2 egg whites
½ cup grated parmesan cheese
¼ teaspoon cayenne pepper
1 teaspoon garlic powder
¼ teaspoon salt
pepper to taste
1 ½ tablespoons butter
2 boneless, skinless chicken breasts, tenderized for even thickness

Preheat oven to 400°.

Grease a broiler pan or a baking pan with a rack with nonstick cooking spray.

Place oat flour in a medium bowl. Place egg whites in a separate medium bowl. In a third medium bowl, combine parmesan cheese, cayenne pepper, garlic powder, salt, and pepper.

Dip chicken into the flour bowl and lightly press to coat each side of the chicken. Next, dip chicken in the egg whites and allow the excess egg to drip off. Finally, place chicken in the parmesan cheese blend and lightly press to coat evenly on both sides.

In a small, microwavable bowl, melt the butter, then drizzle over the top of the chicken.

Place coated chicken on prepared baking rack. Place in oven and bake for 20–23 minutes. Then turn oven off and turn on broil setting, and broil for 2–3 minutes, until top of chicken is light golden brown.

Remove from oven and allow to rest 3 minutes, then serve.

MAKES 2 SERVINGS
Serving size: 4 ounces
Calories: 462
Fat: 20g
Saturated fat: 10g
Polyunsaturated fat: 0.5g
Monounsaturated fat: 2g
Trans fat: 0g
Cholesterol: 44mg
Sodium: 810mg
Carbohydrates: 12g
Fiber: 1.5g
Sugar: 0.5g
Protein: 43g
Iron: 5g
Potassium: 127mg

Spinach Feta Burgers

1 pound 93/7 lean ground beef
¼ teaspoon salt
¼ teaspoon pepper
½ teaspoon cayenne pepper
1 teaspoon fresh garlic, minced
4 ounces fresh baby spinach, chopped
4 ounces feta cheese crumbles
4 whole wheat hamburger buns

In a medium bowl, combine beef, salt, pepper, cayenne pepper, and garlic. Mix until all ingredients are combined. Next, gently fold in the spinach and feta cheese crumbles.

Form 4 burger patties, then lightly press the center of the burger to make a dent in it. This will help keep the burgers from shrinking and puffing up in the center.

Heat a grill pan or cast-iron skillet over medium-high heat. Once hot, place burgers down, allowing 1 inch of space between them. Cook on each side 3–4 minutes. Do not press down on burgers. You want those delicious juices to remain intact. Once burgers are done, move to a plate and allow them to rest 2–3 minutes before serving to let the juices absorb back into the meat.

Place on hamburger bun and enjoy. If following a low-carb diet, omit bun for 2–4 large romaine lettuce leaves to serve as the bun.

MAKES 4 BURGER PORTIONS WITH BUN
Serving size: 4-ounce burger
Calories: 399
Fat: 15g
Saturated fat: 6g
Polyunsaturated fat: 1g
Monounsaturated fat: 0g
Trans fat: 0g
Cholesterol: 90mg
Sodium: 702mg
Carbohydrates: 32g
Fiber: 3g
Sugar: 2g
Protein: 33g
Iron: 29g
Potassium: 676mg

Low-Carb Steak Fajitas

1 ½ tablespoons low-sodium soy sauce
1 tablespoon red wine vinegar
2 teaspoons Worcestershire sauce
2 teaspoons lemon juice
1 tablespoon olive oil
1 teaspoon fresh garlic, minced
¼ teaspoon pepper
8-ounce flank steak
nonstick cooking spray
¼ red bell pepper
¼ green bell pepper
¼ white onion
4 large romaine leaves

In a medium bowl, combine soy sauce, red wine vinegar, Worcestershire, lemon juice, olive oil, garlic, and pepper. Whisk until combined.

Place steak in a shallow pan and pour half the marinade over the steak. Turn steak over and pour the remaining marinade over the steak. Cover and place in the fridge for 6–8 hours.

Preheat grill pan or outdoor grill on medium-high heat. Spray with the nonstick cooking spray. Once grill is hot, place meat on grill and save marinade for vegetables. Allow steak to grill for 4–5 minutes per side or until steak is cooked to your desire.

Remove steak from grill and place on cutting board. Let rest 5–7 minutes.

While steak rests, slice the red and green bell peppers and onion into thin strips. Place into a skillet over high heat with 3-4 tablespoons of the marinade. Allow veggies to cook down until soft, yet firm in texture.

Slice steak into thin strips and add to the pan with the vegetables. Stir to combine, then spoon into romaine leaves and enjoy!

MAKES 2 SERVINGS
Serving size: 4 ounces steak
Calories: 289
Fat: 15g
Saturated fat: 5g
Polyunsaturated fat: 0g
Monounsaturated fat: 5g
Trans fat: 0g
Cholesterol: 75mg
Sodium: 575mg
Carbohydrates: 9.5g
Fiber: 1.5g
Sugar: 9g
Protein: 27g
Iron: 18.5g
Potassium: 246m

Sriracha Shrimp Tacos

1 pound shrimp, 26–30 count (fresh or frozen)
1 ½ cup red or green cabbage, shredded
1 jalapeño pepper, seeded and diced
pinch of pepper
pinch of salt
1 tablespoon honey
1 lime, juiced and zested
¼ cup plain nonfat greek yogurt
1 tablespoon sriracha sauce
1 teaspoon garlic powder
1 teaspoon paprika
¼ teaspoon dried red pepper flakes
6 corn tortillas
nonstick cooking spray
2 tablespoons fresh cilantro, chopped

Thaw, clean, and peel the shrimp. Chop into thirds and set aside.

In a medium bowl, combine the cabbage shreds, jalapeño, salt, pepper, and honey. Mix well. Add in half the lime juice and toss together.

In a small bowl, combine greek yogurt and sriracha sauce and mix well.

In additional small bowl combine garlic powder, paprika, red pepper flakes, and a dash of salt and pepper. This will be your shrimp seasoning.

Spray a large skillet with nonstick cooking spray and set over medium heat. When pan is heated, add in shrimp. Cook for 1 minute, then sprinkle with half of the seasoning mix. Flip shrimp over and sprinkle the other side. Add remaining lime juice to pan. Continue to cook for 2–3 minutes, until shrimp become opaque in color and pink.

Divide shrimp into corn tortillas, sprinkle with cilantro, and add a drizzle of the yogurt sriracha sauce. Top with cabbage mixture and a dash of the lime zest.

MAKES 6 TACOS
Serving size: 1 taco
Calories: 158
Fat: 2g
Saturated fat: 0g
Polyunsaturated fat: 0g
Monounsaturated fat: 0g
Trans fat: 0g
Cholesterol: 0mg
Sodium: 63mg
Carbohydrates: 16.5g
Fiber: 3g
Sugar: 5g
Protein: 16.5g
Iron: 3g
Potassium: 79mg

Salted Caramel Latte Smoothie

- ½ cup unsweetened almond milk
- ½ frozen banana
- 1 scoop 1stPhorm Level-1 Caramel Latte protein powder
- ¼ cup plain nonfat Greek yogurt
- 1 teaspoon Stevia
- ¼ cup oats
- pinch of sea salt

Layer all ingredients in a blender from liquid to solid, then blend until smooth. For a thinner or thicker texture, add more or a little less almond milk.

MAKES 1 SMOOTHIE
Calories: 296
Fat: 6g
Saturated fat: 2g
Poly unSaturated fat: 1g
Monounsaturated fat: 1g
Trans fat: 0g
Cholesterol: 62mg
Sodium: 209mg
Carbohydrates: 27g
Fiber: 3g
Sugar: 8g
Protein: 31g
Iron: 7g
Potassium: 199mg

Blueberry Pie Smoothie

½ cup plain nonfat Greek yogurt
½ cup frozen blueberries
½ cup frozen banana
¼ cup oats
¼ teaspoon lemon juice
½ cup unsweetened almond milk
1 scoop 1stPhorm Level-1 Vanilla Ice Cream protein powder

Layer all ingredients in a blender from liquid to solid, then blend until smooth. For a thinner or thicker texture, add more or a little less almond milk.

MAKES 1 SMOOTHIE
Calories: 339
Fat: 6g
Saturated fat: 2g
Polyunsaturated fat: 1g
Monounsaturated fat: 1g
Trans fat: 0g
Cholesterol: 62mg
Sodium: 210mg
Carbohydrates: 38g
Fiber: 5g
Sugar: 5g
Protein: 32g
Iron: 8g
Potassium: 256mg

Chocolate Microwave Bowl Cake

- 1 scoop 1stPhorm Level-1 Milk Chocolate protein powder
- 2 tablespoons cocoa powder
- ½ teaspoon baking powder
- 1 tablespoon coconut flour
- 2 tablespoons Splenda (or Truvia)
- 3 tablespoons liquid egg white
- 1 tablespoon unsweetened applesauce
- ¼ cup unsweetened almond milk
- mini chocolate chips (optional)
- nonstick cooking spray

In a cereal bowl, combine protein powder, cocoa powder, baking powder, coconut flour, and Splenda.

In a mug, combine egg white, applesauce, and almond milk.

Pour the wet ingredients into the dry ingredients and mix until well combined.

Spray another cereal bowl lightly with nonstick cooking spray and pour in cake mix.

Finally, sprinkle the top with mini chocolate chips if you wish.

Place bowl in microwave and heat for 1 minute and 15 seconds. Carefully remove from microwave, as bowl may be hot. Serve warm from the microwave.

MAKES 1 CAKE
Calories: 240
Fat: 6g
Saturated fat: 4g
Polyunsaturated fat: 0g
Monounsaturated fat: 1g
Trans fat: 0g
Cholesterol: 60mg
Sodium: 280mg
Carbohydrates: 16g
Fiber: 7g
Sugar: 4g
Protein: 32g
Iron: 14g
Potassium: 259mg

Pumpkin Spice Doughnuts

FOR DOUGHNUTS

nonstick cooking spray
½ cup 1stPhorm Level-1 Cinnamon Cookie Batter protein powder
¼ cup coconut flour
⅓ cup Stevia
1 teaspoon pumpkin pie spice
1 teaspoon baking powder
½ cup canned pumpkin
2 eggs
¼ cup unsweetened applesauce
6 tablespoons unsweetened almond milk

FOR GLAZE

(you may add glaze or simply toss in a mixture of cinnamon and Stevia)
3 tablespoons coconut oil
4 ½ tablespoons 1stPhorm Cinnamon Cookie Batter protein powder

OPTIONAL TOPPINGS

chocolate, nuts, sprinkles

Preheat oven to 350°.

Spray a 6-doughnut doughnut pan with nonstick cooking spray.

In a medium bowl, combine protein powder, coconut flour, Stevia, pumpkin pie spice, and baking powder. Mix well.

In a large bowl, combine pumpkin, eggs, applesauce, and almond milk. Whisk until smooth.

Pour the dry ingredients into the wet ingredients. Whisk to combine.

Spoon batter into the doughnut pan, filling cavities to the top but not overflowing.

Place pan in the oven and bake 19–21 minutes or until toothpick comes out clean.

Remove from oven and let rest 2–3 minutes. Then turn doughnuts out onto a cooling rack to cool.

In a small bowl, yet large enough to dip doughnuts into, melt the 3 tablespoons of coconut oil. Then slowly stir in the protein powder.

Once doughnuts are completely cooled, carefully dip each doughnut one by one into the glaze, then place back onto the cooling rack and top with any additional toppings. Repeat until all doughnuts are glazed.

Next, place the cooling rack that is holding the doughnuts into the fridge for 10 minutes to allow the glaze to set and firm.

Remove from the fridge and store in an airtight container at room temperature.

MAKES 6 DOUGHNUTS
Serving size: 1 doughnut
Calories: 170
Fat: 10g
Saturated fat: 7g
Polyunsaturated fat: 0g
Monounsaturated fat: 1g
Trans fat: 0g
Cholesterol: 81mg
Sodium: 98mg
Carbohydrates: 7g
Fiber: 2.5g
Sugar: 2.5g
Protein: 11g
Iron: 7g
Potassium: 76mg

Guacamole Stuffed Eggs

6 large hard-boiled eggs, cooled and peeled
2 avocados, pitted and peeled
¼ cup fresh cilantro, chopped
1 tablespoon green onion, green and light green portion only, chopped
1 teaspoon red pepper flakes
1 Roma tomato, chopped
1 tablespoon lime juice
pinch of sea salt
pinch of paprika for garnish

Cut eggs vertically in half and discard yolk.

In a medium bowl, mash together avocados, then stir in cilantro, green onion, red pepper flakes, tomato, lime juice, and sea salt.

Spoon filling into the egg whites. Then sprinkle with paprika for garnish.

Store in the fridge until you're ready to serve.

MAKES 6 SERVINGS
Serving size: 2 halves
Calories: 130
Fat: 7g
Saturated fat: 1g
Polyunsaturated fat: 1g
Monounsaturated fat: 4g
Trans fat: 0g
Cholesterol: 0mg
Sodium: 59mg
Carbohydrates: 6g
Fiber: 4g
Sugar: 1g
Protein: 5g
Iron: 2g
Potassium: 301mg

Kicked-Up Corn

1½ tablespoons extra virgin olive oil
1–2 teaspoons sea salt + 1 pinch
⅛ teaspoon red pepper flakes
⅛ teaspoon fresh cracked black pepper
⅛ teaspoon garlic powder
¼ teaspoon lime juice
4 ears of corn
Optional: 2 tablespoons fresh grated parmesan cheese

In a small dish, combine olive oil, pinch of sea salt, red pepper flakes, black pepper, garlic powder, and lime juice. Mix well until combined.

If you prefer your corn boiled, fill a pot large enough to hold all 4 ears of corn ⅔ full of water. Add 1–2 teaspoons of sea salt to the water, place on the stove, and bring water to a boil. Once you have a roaring boil, carefully add the ears of corn. Allow water to return to boil and let corn boil 5–7 minutes. When corn is done boiling, remove it from the water and place on a paper towel to absorb excess water. Plate corn and, using a basting brush, brush olive oil mixture over corn. Sprinkle with the parmesan cheese if desired, and enjoy!

If you prefer your corn grilled, place ears of corn on individual sheets of foil. Brush with olive oil mixture and wrap ear of corn with foil, being sure foil is completely closed. Place over heat on the grill and cook about 15 minutes, turning frequently. Remove from grill and use caution when unwrapping foil so the steam doesn't burn you. Sprinkle with parmesan if desired, and dig in!

MAKES 4 SERVINGS
Serving size: 1 ear of corn
Calories: 116
Fat: 6g
Saturated fat: 0g
Polyunsaturated fat: 1g
Monounsaturated fat: 3g
Trans fat: 0g
Cholesterol: 0mg
Sodium: 740mg
Protein: 2g
Carbohydrates: 17g
Fiber: 2g
Sugar: 2g
Iron: 2g
Potassium: 191mg

Roasted Broccolini & Carrots

3 cups cleaned and trimmed broccolini
1 ½ cup carrots, peeled and sliced
1 tablespoon olive oil
2 cloves fresh garlic, minced
2 tablespoons fresh parmesan cheese shreds
salt to taste
pepper to taste

Preheat oven to 400°.

Line a baking sheet with foil.

In a medium bowl, combine broccolini, carrots, olive oil, and garlic. Toss to coat evenly, then pour onto prepared baking sheet and spread evenly.

Sprinkle on parmesan cheese, salt, and pepper. Place in oven and bake 17–20 minutes.

*To create a lower-fat option, simply place veggies on baking pan, then spray with nonstick cooking spray in place of olive oil and sprinkle with the garlic, salt, pepper, and parmesan cheese.

MAKES 2 SERVINGS
Serving size: 2 cups
Calories: 153
Fat: 10g
Saturated fat: 2g
Polyunsaturated fat: 1g
Monounsaturated fat: 5g
Trans fat: 0g
Cholesterol: 3.5mg
Sodium: 161mg
Carbohydrates: 15g
Fiber: 6g
Sugar: 6g
Protein: 4.5g
Iron: 6g
Potassium: 673mg

Garlic Herb Roasted Potatoes

- nonstick cooking spray
- 1 pound small red potatoes, scrubbed and cut in half
- 1 tablespoon olive oil
- 2 cloves fresh garlic, minced
- ½ teaspoon black pepper
- ¾ teaspoon sea salt
- ¼ teaspoon dried thyme
- ¾ teaspoon dried basil
- ¼ teaspoon dried oregano
- ⅛ cup grated parmesan cheese

Preheat oven to 400°.

Spray a baking sheet with nonstick spray, or line with foil first, and then spray with nonstick spray for an easy clean-up.

In a large bowl, mix the potatoes, olive oil, garlic, pepper, salt, thyme, basil, oregano, and parmesan cheese. Toss until potatoes are evenly coated.

Pour potatoes out onto baking sheet and spread evenly. Place in oven and bake for 40–45 minutes or until tender when pricked with a fork.

Remove from oven and serve.

MAKES 4 SERVINGS
Serving size: 1 cup
Calories: 127
Fat: 4g
Saturated fat: 1g
Polyunsaturated fat: 0g
Monounsaturated fat: 2.5
Trans fat: 0g
Cholesterol: 1.75mg
Sodium: 382mg
Carbohydrates: 20g
Fiber: 2g
Sugar: 1g
Protein: 3g
Iron: 6.5g

Cauliflower Whip

1 large or 2 small heads of cauliflower, washed, cleaned, and cut into florets
⅓ cup green onions, just green and light green portion, chopped
⅓ cup shredded cheddar cheese
2 tablespoons butter
1 teaspoon garlic powder
sea salt to taste
pepper to taste

In a large microwave-safe dish, add the cauliflower florets and cover tightly with plastic wrap. Microwave for 8–10 minutes until tender.

When cauliflower is done, carefully pull back plastic wrap. Be careful, as the steam can burn you.

Transfer the cauliflower to your food processor (or a bowl with a hand mixer). Add in the remaining ingredients. Run on high setting for 30 seconds, then pulse to ensure all cauliflower is whipped well.

Serve immediately.

MAKES 4 SERVINGS
Serving size: 1 cup
Calories: 82
Fat: 2.5g
Saturated fat: 1g
Polyunsaturated fat: 0g
Monounsaturated fat: 0.5g
Trans fat: 0g
Cholesterol: 8mg
Sodium: 212mg
Carbohydrates: 9g
Fiber: 4g
Sugar: 4.5g
Protein: 6.5g
Iron: 4g
Potassium: 577mg

Simple Baked Veggies

- nonstick cooking spray
- 1 large zucchini, sliced into quarters
- 1 large yellow squash, sliced into quarters
- ½ cup cherry tomatoes, sliced in half
- 1 cup whole mushrooms, sliced in half
- ¼ cup white onion, minced
- 1 teaspoon Italian seasoning
- ½ teaspoon garlic powder
- salt to taste
- pepper to taste
- 2 tablespoons parmesan cheese, grated

Preheat oven to 350°

Spray an 8-by-8-inch baking dish with nonstick cooking spray.

Place all ingredients except the parmesan cheese in a medium bowl and mix well to combine and coat evenly.

Place into baking dish and sprinkle with parmesan cheese.

Bake for 25–30 minutes or until tender.

MAKES 4 SERVINGS
Serving size: 1 cup
Calories: 42
Fat: 1.5g
Saturated fat: 0g
Polyunsaturated fat: 0g
Monounsaturated fat: 0g
Trans fat: 0g
Cholesterol: 3.5mg
Sodium: 73mg
Carbohydrates: 5.5g
Fiber: 1.5g
Sugar: 3.5g
Protein: 3g
Iron: 2.5g
Potassium: 333mg

Cauliflower Crisps

4 cups cauliflower florets
2 eggs, lightly beaten
¾ cup Panko bread crumbs
1 teaspoon garlic powder
½ cup grated parmesan cheese
salt to taste
pepper to taste

Preheat oven to 400°.

Line a baking sheet with parchment paper.

Clean cauliflower and cut into bite-sized pieces.

In a small bowl, add the beaten eggs. In a second bowl, combine the bread crumbs, garlic powder, and parmesan cheese.

Dip cauliflower into the egg mixture, allowing excess to drip off. Then dip into breadcrumbs mixture.

Place coated cauliflower on the baking sheet, then sprinkle with salt and pepper. Bake for 20–25 minutes or until cauliflower is tender.

MAKES 4 SERVINGS
Serving size: 1 cup
Calories: 157
Fat: 6g
Saturated fat: 3g
Polyunsaturated fat: 0g
Monounsaturated fat: 2g
Trans fat: 0g
Cholesterol: 103mg
Sodium: 271mg
Carbohydrates: 15g
Fiber: 3g
Sugar: 3g
Protein: 11g
Iron: 6g
Potassium: 362mg

Roasted Balsamic Carrots & Mushrooms

½ pound carrots peeled and chopped
1 pound whole mushrooms cut in half
1 tablespoon olive oil
3 tablespoons balsamic vinegar
2 tablespoons low-sodium soy sauce
2 cloves of fresh garlic, minced
¼ teaspoon dried thyme
salt to taste
pepper to taste

Preheat oven to 400°.

In a medium bowl combine the carrots, mushrooms, olive oil, balsamic vinegar, soy sauce, garlic, and thyme.

Line a baking sheet with parchment paper. Pour mixture onto baking sheet and spread evenly.

Bake for 12 minutes, then stir and bake an additional 8 minutes. Add salt and pepper to taste.

MAKES 4 SERVINGS
Serving size: 1 cup
Calories: 100
Fat: 3g
Saturated fat: 0g
Polyunsaturated fat: 0g
Monounsaturated fat: 2.5g
Trans fat: 0g
Cholesterol: 8mg
Sodium: 396mg
Carbohydrates: 12.5g
Fiber: 2.5g
Sugar: 8g
Protein: 5g
Iron: 6g
Potassium: 380mg

Note: Page numbers in italics indicate photographs.

INDEX

INDEX

Note: Page numbers in italics indicate photographs.

Loaded Breakfast Burrito

8 eggs
2 tablespoons of milk
salt to taste
pepper to taste
nonstick cooking spray
6 (10-inch) tortillas
1 ½ cups cheddar cheese
1 cup pepper jack cheese
1 pound ground sausage, cooked and drained
½ pound bacon, cooked
1 jalapeño, seeded and diced
3 Roma tomatoes, diced

Heat a skillet over low-medium heat and spray with nonstick cooking spray. In a medium bowl, whisk together eggs, milk, salt, and pepper. Add egg mixture to skillet and cook just until done.

Sprinkle tortillas with the cheeses and add in a few tablespoons of the scrambled eggs. Then add in the sausage, bacon, jalapeños, and tomatoes. Fold in sides and roll up tight.

Place completed burritos on a microwave-safe platter and cover with a lightly damp paper towel. Microwave for 15–30 seconds, until cheese is just melted.

MAKES 6 BURRITOS
Serving size: 1 burrito
Calories: 730
Fat: 49g
Saturated fat: 20g
Polyunsaturated fat: 2g
Monounsaturated fat: 5.5g
Trans fat: 0g
Cholesterol: 306mg
Sodium: 2,258mg
Carbohydrates: 29g
Fiber: 1.5g
Sugar: 2.5g
Protein: 43g
Iron: 28g
Potassium: 183.5mg

Loaded Potato Wedges

2 pounds wedged Russet potatoes
3 tablespoons olive oil
1 teaspoon salt
1 teaspoon pepper
½ teaspoon garlic powder
½ cup shredded cheddar cheese
⅓ cup cooked crisp bacon, crumbled
¼ cup green onion tops, chopped
¼ cup sour cream

Preheat oven to 400°.

In a large bowl, add in wedged potatoes and drizzle with olive oil, then sprinkle with salt, pepper, and garlic powder. Toss potatoes until equally coated with mixture.

Lay potato wedges on parchment-lined baking sheet and bake at 400° for 15–20 minutes, then remove from oven, flip onto opposite side, and bake for another 15–20 minutes.

Remove potato wedges from oven and arrange them close together on pan to hold all the toppings. Sprinkle wedges with cheddar cheese, bacon, and chopped onions, then return to oven for 5 minutes or until cheese is melted. Remove from oven and top with sour cream and serve.

MAKES 6 SERVINGS
Serving size: 5 ounces
Calories: 334
Fat: 13g
Saturated fat: 4g
Polyunsaturated fat: 1g
Monounsaturated fat: 7g
Trans fat: 0g
Cholesterol: 16.5mg
Sodium: 158mg
Carbohydrates: 48g
Fiber: 4g
Sugar: 2g
Protein: 9g
Iron: 12g
Potassium: 1171mg

Caprese Grilled Cheese

nonstick cooking spray
1 tablespoon butter
2 slices thick-sliced bread
3 ounces fresh mozzarella
4 slices Roma tomatoes
1–2 tablespoons fresh basil, chopped
salt to taste
pepper to taste

Heat a medium sized skillet over medium heat. Spray with nonstick cooking spray.

Spread butter evenly on one side of each slice of bread.

Place one slice of bread, butter side down, in warmed skillet. Then layer with the cheese, tomato, and basil and sprinkle with salt and pepper. Place remaining bread slice butter side up and allow to cook for 2–3 minutes or until bread is light-golden brown. Then gently flip the sandwich over so that the remaining butter side of bread is on the skillet. Cook for 2–3 minutes until light-golden brown and cheese is melted.

Remove from skillet and allow to rest 1 minute before enjoying.

MAKES 1 SANDWICH
Calories: 544
Fat: 29g
Saturated fat: 16g
Polyunsaturated fat: 0g
Monounsaturated fat: 3g
Trans fat: 0g
Cholesterol: 91mg
Sodium: 720mg
Carbohydrates: 44g
Fiber: 3g
Sugar: 5g
Protein: 21g
Iron: 13g
Potassium: 19mg

Chocolate Fluff Dip

¾ cup Nutella
1 (13-ounce) jar of marshmallow fluff
Fruit and cookie dippers of your choice

In a medium bowl, combine Nutella and marshmallow fluff using a hand mixer on medium speed. Blend until smooth and combined. Transfer to a serving dish and serve with your choice of dippers.

Some of my favorites are fresh fruit, Rice Krispie treats, cookies, and graham crackers.

MAKES 2 CUPS
Serving size: 2 tablespoons
Calories: 139
Fat: 3g
Saturated fat: 1.5g
Polyunsaturated fat: 0g
Monounsaturated fat: 0g
Trans fat: 0g
Cholesterol: 0mg
Sodium: 3.5mg
Carbohydrates: 27g
Fiber: 0g
Sugar: 21g
Protein :0g
Iron: 1.5g
Potassium: 0mg

Loaded Breakfast Waffle

5 eggs
¼ cup milk
½ cup cooked sausage, crumbled
1 cup shredded cheddar cheese
¼ cup green onions, chopped
salt to taste
pepper to taste
1 (20-ounce) bag pre-shredded hash browns
nonstick cooking spray or butter

In a medium mixing bowl, combine eggs, milk, sausage, cheese, green onions, salt, and pepper. Once ingredients are well combined, stir in the hash browns.

Heat waffle iron on medium-high setting and spray with nonstick cooking spray or brush with melted butter.

Scoop approximately 1 cup of the mixture onto your waffle iron and spread, keeping it 1 inch away from edges. Close waffle iron and cook for 5–7 minutes, checking every few minutes to ensure it doesn't burn.

Remove the waffle with a fork or tongs.

MAKES 4 WAFFLES
Serving size: 1 waffle
Calories: 470
Fat: 30g
Saturated fat: 12g
Polyunsaturated fat: 2g
Monounsaturated fat: 9g
Trans fat: 0g
Cholesterol: 256mg
Sodium: 882mg
Carbohydrates: 31g
Fiber: 2.5g
Sugar: 2.5g
Protein: 22g
Iron: 20g
Potassium: 577mg

Using a small bowl, combine the cinnamon, pecans, butter, and brown sugar for the filling. Fold half of the filling mixture into the muffin batter.

Fill muffin cups about ⅓ full with batter. Top with remaining topping mixture. Bake at 400° for 12–15 minutes. Remove from oven and allow to set for 5 minutes, then transfer to cooling rack.

In a small bowl, whisk together all the icing ingredients, then drizzle or pipe over the muffins.

MAKES 12 MUFFINS

Serving size: 1 muffin
Calories: 332
Fat: 14g
Saturated fat: 4.5g
Polyunsaturated fat: 2g
Monounsaturated fat: 5g
Trans fat: 0g
Cholesterol: 34mg
Sodium: 91mg
Protein: 5g
Carbohydrates: 48g
Fiber: 1.5g
Sugar: 32g
Iron: 2g
Potassium: 119mg

Chocolate Chip Muffins

paper muffin liners or nonstick cooking spray
2 cups all-purpose flour
½ cup sugar
1 tablespoon of baking powder
½ teaspoon salt
1 egg
¾ cup milk
⅓ cup vegetable oil
¾ cup mini chocolate chips

Preheat oven to 400°.

Line a muffin tin with paper liners or spray with nonstick cooking spray.

In a large bowl combine the flour, sugar, baking powder, and salt.

In a small bowl, beat the egg, milk, and oil.

Stir the wet ingredients into the dry ingredients just until moistened. Fold in the chocolate chips.

Fill muffin cups ¾ full. Bake for 18–20 minutes, until a toothpick comes out clean.

Place muffins onto cooling rack and allow to cool, then store in an airtight container at room temperature.

MAKES 4 MUFFINS
Serving size: 1 muffin
Calories: 248
Fat: 11g
Saturated fat: 4g
Polyunsaturated fat: 4g
Monounsaturated fat: 1g
Trans fat: 0g
Cholesterol: 18mg
Sodium: 111mg
Carbohydrates: 34g
Fiber: 1g
Sugar: 17g
Protein: 4g
Iron: 0g
Potassium: 56mg

Melt butter and shortening in a small saucepan and stir to combine. Remove from heat and set aside.

In a large bowl, whisk together the flour, baking powder, sugar, and salt and set aside.

In a medium bowl, whisk together the eggs, milk, chocolate syrup, and vanilla extract. Whisk the egg mixture into the flour mixture until well combined. Batter will be slightly lumpy. Next, whisk in the butter mixture until combined.

Preheat the oven to 250° with a baking sheet in the oven as it preheats. To keep waffles warm while working on each batch, place them on this sheet until they are all ready to serve.

Preheat your waffle iron and spray with nonstick cooking spray if needed. (Some waffle irons are nonstick.)

Pour enough batter into the waffle iron to come within an inch of the sides. Cook until fluffy. Place the waffle on the hot baking sheet and repeat until batter is gone.

To serve, plate and top with your favorite toppings and additional chocolate syrup.

MAKES 4 WAFFLES

Serving size: 1 waffle
Calories: 463
Fat: 23g
Saturated fat: 10g
Polyunsaturated fat: 5.5g
Monounsaturated fat: 5.5g
Trans fat: 0g
Cholesterol: 167mg
Sodium: 479mg
Carbohydrates: 54g
Fiber: 1.5g
Sugar: 30g
Protein: 10g
Iron: 6g
Potassium: 261mg

Fold the wet mixture into the dry mixture just until combined.

Spread the batter in a 9-by-5-inch loaf pan lightly greased with nonstick cooking spray.

Bake 50–55 minutes or until a toothpick comes out clean. Place pan onto cooling rack and cool for 30 minutes, then turn loaf out onto cooling rack and continue to cool.

Once cooled, prepare the glaze in a small bowl by whisking all ingredients together. Then pour or spoon over the top of the bread. Allow to set for 20 minutes to dry. Slice into 10 pieces and serve.

MAKES 10 SERVINGS

Serving size: 1 slice
Calories: 500
Fat: 22g
Saturated fat: 13g
Polyunsaturated fat: 0g
Monounsaturated fat: 2g
Trans fat: 0g
Cholesterol: 62mg
Sodium: 168mg
Carbohydrates: 69g
Fiber: 4g
Sugar: 51g
Protein: 7.5g
Iron: 19g
Potassium: 120mg

1 (3-pound) beef chuck roast
1 (2-ounce) packet of dried onion soup mix
1 ½ pounds small red potatoes
3 cups carrots, coarsely chopped, or whole baby carrots
salt and pepper to taste

Place roast in crockpot. Sprinkle top and sides of roast with dry onion soup mix.

Place potatoes around the bottom of the roast, then top with carrots. Sprinkle salt and pepper around the vegetables.

Cover and cook on low for 6–8 hours or high 4–6 hours

MAKES 6 SERVINGS
Serving size: 6oz of roast & 4oz potatoes & veggies
Calories: 468
Fat: 11g
Saturated fat: 0g
Polyunsaturated fat: 0g
Monounsaturated fat: 0g
Trans fat: 0g
Cholesterol: 120mg
Sodium: 655mg
Carbohydrates: 36g
Fiber: 4g
Sugar: 4g
Protein: 54g
Iron: 32g
Potassium: 1584mg

Chocolate Peanut Butter Pie

1 cup plus 3 tablespoons peanut butter*, divided
½ cup sugar
1 cup cream cheese, softened
4½ cups Cool Whip, divided (1 ½, 8oz containers)
1 prepared chocolate pie crust
1 (11-ounce) jar of hot fudge ice cream topping, divided

In a large bowl, beat together 1 cup peanut butter, sugar, and cream cheese until smooth. Gently mix in 3 cups of Cool Whip until combined.

Spoon peanut butter mixture into prepared crust.

Reserve 3 tablespoons of hot fudge topping in a small sandwich bag, then place the hot fudge jar in the microwave and heat for 1 minute. Stir well, then pour onto top of peanut butter mixture and spread evenly. Place pie in the fridge and allow it to set for 10 minutes.

Remove pie from fridge and cover with remaining Cool Whip.

Place hot fudge bag in microwave for 10 seconds to soften, then snip the corner off and pipe onto top of Cool Whip. Repeat with 3 tablespoons peanut butter.

Refrigerate for at least 2 hours. May be made 2 days ahead.

*Don't use natural peanut butter, due to oil separation.

MAKES 8 SERVINGS
Serving size: ⅛ of pie
Calories: 688
Fat: 42g
Saturated fat: 16g
Polyunsaturated fat:0g
Monounsaturated fat: 0g
Trans fat: 0g
Cholesterol: 35mg
Sodium: 378mg
Carbohydrates: 63g
Fiber: 4g
Sugar: 49g
Protein: 13g
Iron: 15g
Potassium: 234mg

1 package Oreos
½ cup butter
1 cup powdered sugar
8 ounces cream cheese
6 cups Cool Whip, divided
2 (3.4-ounce) boxes instant chocolate pudding
4 cups milk

Place Oreos in a large Ziploc bag and crush using a rolling pin. (Alternatively, use a food processor.) Once crushed, reserve ¾ cup for topping.

In a microwave-safe bowl, melt the butter.

Pour butter into a 9-by-13-inch baking pan and add in remaining crumbs. Mix well until crumbs and butter are combined. Pat firmly into the bottom of the pan to create the crust.

In a medium bowl, mix the powdered sugar, cream cheese, and half the Cool Whip with a hand mixer until smooth. Spread over the Oreo crust.

Next, make the chocolate pudding according to its instructions, using the milk.

Spread the chocolate pudding over the top, and finally top with the remaining Cool Whip and sprinkle with reserved Oreo crumbs.

Place in the refrigerator to chill for at least 4 hours. May be made 2 days ahead.

MAKES 12 SERVINGS
Serving size: 1/12 cheesecake
Calories: 538
Fat: 27g
Saturated fat: 15g
Polyunsaturated fat: 1g
Monounsaturated fat: 5g
Trans fat: 0g
Cholesterol :50mg
Sodium: 626mg
Carbohydrates: 53g
Fiber: 1g
Sugar: 47g
Protein: 5g
Iron: 18g
Potassium: 201mg

oil egg noodles in a large saucepan.
crockpot, and gently stir into the soup to

MAKES 12 SERVINGS

Serving size: 1 ½ cups
Calories: 163
Fat: 6g
Saturated fat: 1g
Polyunsaturated fat: 1g
Monounsaturated fat: 2g
Trans fat: 0g
Cholesterol: 33mg
Sodium: 1339mg
Carbohydrates: 16g
Fiber: 2.5g
Sugar: 2g
Protein: 10g
Iron: 4.5g
Potassium: 219mg

Baked Potato Soup

9 medium-large russet potatoes
⅔ cup butter
⅔ cup all-purpose flour
6 cups whole milk
1 ½ cups cheddar cheese, shredded, plus extra for topping
⅓ cup bacon bits, plus extra for topping
1½ tablespoons green onions, chopped, plus extra for topping
½ tablespoon salt
1 teaspoon pepper
8 ounces sour cream

Poke holes in potatoes with a fork to vent and place on a microwave-safe plate. Microwave potatoes until tender (about 5 minutes per side, but times will vary based on microwave), then scoop out the flesh and chop up the skins.

In a large saucepan over medium heat, melt butter. Stir in flour and cook for 1 minute. Whisk in milk a little bit at a time, stirring constantly until thickened.

Stir in potatoes, chopped peels, cheese, bacon bits, green onions, salt, and pepper.

Cook until heated throughout. Stir in sour cream and heat through.

Serve topped with extra bacon bits, green onions, and cheese.

MAKES 12 SERVINGS
Serving size: 1 ½ cups
Calories: 380
Fat: 25g
Saturated fat: 1.5g
Polyunsaturated fat: 1g
Monounsaturated fat: 6g
Trans fat: 0g
Cholesterol: 69.5mg
Sodium: 526mg
Carbohydrates: 26g
Fiber: 1.5g
Sugar: 7.5g
Protein: 12g
Iron: 5g
Potassium: 704mg

Cast-Iron Skillet Steak

2 (6-ounce) steak cuts of your choice
2 teaspoons of garlic powder
1½ teaspoons sea salt
1 teaspoon ground pepper
2 tablespoons of butter, divided

Place steaks on a plate and allow to come to room temperature for 20–30 minutes before cooking.

Using a cast-iron pan or skillet, heat over high heat to get the skillet super hot. To test the temperature, sprinkle with a few drops of water. Water should sizzle and "dance" when the skillet is ready.

Sprinkle both sides of steaks with garlic, salt, and pepper.

Place steaks in the center portion of the skillet or pan and gently press down to ensure a good seat in the pan. Set your time for the desired cook, listed below. Once time is over, flip steaks and again gently press for a well-seated steak. Time this once again to ensure desired preference. When steaks are done, turn heat off and add a half tablespoon butter to the top of each steak. Place the rest in the bottom of the skillet near the steaks. Let it simmer for 30 seconds.

Remove steaks and plate onto serving dishes. Tilt skillet to the side and allow butter and juices to gather into one side. Using a spoon, spoon liquid onto the top of the plated steaks for extra flavor.

Allow steaks to rest 5 minutes before serving.

Steak Cook Times:

RARE: Cook 5 minutes on one side, 3 minutes on the other. MEDIUM RARE: Cook 5 minutes on one side, 4 minutes on the other.
MEDIUM: Cook 6 minutes on one side, 4 minutes on the other.
MEDIUM WELL: Cook 6 minutes on one side, 5 minutes on the other.
WELL DONE: Cook 8 minutes on one side, 6 minutes on the other.

MAKES 2 SERVINGS
Serving size: 1 steak
Calories: 464
Fat: 30g
Saturated fat: 17g
Polyunsaturated fat: 0g
Monounsaturated fat: 0g
Trans fat: 0g
Cholesterol: 135mg
Sodium: 1411mg
Carbohydrates: 2g
Fiber: 0.5g
Sugar: 0g
Protein: 44g
Iron: 16g
Potassium: 33.5mg

Grandma's Cornbread

½ cup butter plus extra for greasing pan
⅔ cup sugar
2 eggs
1 cup buttermilk
½ teaspoon baking soda
1 cup cornmeal
1 cup all-purpose flour
½ teaspoon salt

Preheat oven to 375°.

Melt butter in large skillet. Remove from heat and stir in sugar. Quickly add eggs and beat until well blended.

Combine buttermilk with baking soda and stir into mixture in skillet. Stir in the cornmeal, flour, and salt until well blended and few lumps remain.

Pour batter into greased 8-inch square pan.

Bake for 30–35 minutes, until a toothpick inserted comes out clean. Cut into 12 squares.

MAKES 12 SERVINGS
Serving size: 1 square
Calories: 202
Fat: 9g
Saturated fat: 5g
Polyunsaturated fat: 0.5g
Monounsaturated fat: 2g
Trans fat: 0g
Cholesterol: 52mg
Sodium: 217mg
Carbohydrates: 27g
Fiber: 1g
Sugar: 11g
Protein: 4g
Iron: 2.5g
Potassium: 43mg

Mac & Cheesy Crunch

FOR MAC AND CHEESE

- ½ pound tubular pasta (measured dry)
- 3 tablespoons butter, plus more for greasing
- ¼ cup flour
- 2 cups whole milk
- 2 teaspoons of hot sauce
- 2 teaspoons of Worcestershire sauce
- ½ teaspoon dry ground mustard powder
- ½ teaspoon salt
- ⅛ teaspoon black pepper
- ⅛ teaspoon cayenne pepper
- pinch of nutmeg
- 2 cups grated extra sharp white cheddar cheese
- ¾ cup shredded parmesan cheese

FOR CRUNCH TOPPING

- ¾ cup crushed potato chips
- 2 cups grated parmesan cheese
- 1 cup extra sharp white cheddar cheese
- 5 slices bacon, crumbled
- parsley (optional)

Heat oven to 375°. Butter a 3-quart casserole dish.

Bring a large pot of generously salted water to a boil and cook the pasta according to the instructions on the package.

Melt the butter in a large saucepan over medium heat. Add the flour and cook, stirring for 1 minute. Whisk in the milk and bring to a simmer, whisking constantly.

Stir the hot sauce, Worcestershire sauce, mustard powder, salt, black pepper, cayenne, and nutmeg into the thickened milk. Stir in cheddar cheese and parmesan cheese until the cheeses melt.

Add the cooked pasta to the cheese sauce and fold together, being careful to not break the noodles. Pour the cheese and noodle mixture into the prepared casserole dish.

To make topping: In a medium bowl, mix together the chips, parmesan cheese, cheddar cheese, bacon, and parsley. Sprinkle the mixture on top of the mac and cheese and bake for 35 minutes. For a crunchier topping, finish under the broiler for 2–3 minutes until golden brown and crisp. Remove from oven and let cool 5 minutes before serving.

MAKES 8 SERVINGS
Serving size: 1 cup
Calories: 506
Fat: 30g
Saturated fat: 17g
Polyunsaturated fat: 1g
Monounsaturated fat: 3g
Trans fat: 0g
Cholesterol: 66mg
Sodium: 841mg
Carbohydrates: 30g
Fiber: 1g
Sugar: 4g
Protein: 28.5g
Iron: 3g
Potassium: 241mg

½ cup butter or margarine
1 cup chopped onion
1 cup chopped celery
6 ounces sliced mushrooms
2 tablespoons chopped fresh parsley
6 cups dry bread cubes
½ teaspoon poultry seasoning
¾ teaspoon dried sage
½ teaspoon dried thyme
¼ teaspoon dried marjoram
¾ teaspoon salt
¼ teaspoon ground black pepper
2 ¼ cups chicken broth, or as needed
1 egg, beaten

Melt butter or margarine in skillet over medium heat. Cook onion, celery, mushroom, and parsley in butter, stirring frequently.

Spoon cooked vegetables over bread cubes in a very large mixing bowl. Season with poultry seasoning, sage, thyme, marjoram, salt, and pepper.

Pour enough of the broth to moisten, and mix in egg. Transfer mixture to slow cooker and cover.

Cook on high for 45 minutes, then reduce heat to low and cook for 4–8 hours.

MAKES 8 SERVINGS
Serving size: 1 cup
Calories: 240
Fat: 13g
Saturated fat: 7g
Polyunsaturated fat: 0g
Monounsaturated fat: 3.5g
Trans fat: 0g
Cholesterol: 54mg
Sodium: 517mg
Carbohydrates: 10g
Fiber: 4g
Sugar: 2g
Protein: 5g
Iron: 35g
Potassium: 566mg

Easy Apple Dumplings

2 large Granny Smith apples
2 (8-count) cans refrigerated crescent roll dough
2 sticks of butter
1 ½ cups brown sugar
1 teaspoon cinnamon
1 teaspoon vanilla extract
1 (12-ounce) can of lemon-lime soda

Preheat oven to 350°.

Wash and slice apples into 8 wedges each.

Butter a 9-by-13-inch baking pan. Unwrap crescent rolls and separate into triangles. Place a piece of the apple on the wide side of the triangle dough and roll to cover apple.

In a separate bowl, combine the butter, brown sugar, cinnamon, and vanilla. Microwave for 30 seconds and mix until you get a liquid mixture without lumps, then spoon the mixture over the rolls.

Pour the soda between the rolls but not over them. Bake for 35–45 minutes, until they become golden brown.

Drizzle pan drippings over the top and serve immediately. This is great paired with classic vanilla ice cream.

MAKES 8 SERVINGS
Serving size: 2 rolls
Calories: 807
Fat: 56g
Saturated fat: 33g
Polyunsaturated fat: 2g
Monounsaturated fat: 12g
Trans fat: 0g
Cholesterol: 122mg
Sodium: 766mg
Carbohydrates: 76g
Fiber: 1g
Sugar: 56g
Protein: 5g
Iron: 6g
Potassium: 70mg

Savory Green Beans

6 slices bacon, chopped
½ cup white onions, chopped
1 teaspoon fresh garlic, minced
1 pound fresh green beans
1 cup water (slightly more if needed)
salt and pepper to taste

Heat a large skillet over medium heat. Once hot, place bacon in skillet and allow fat to render. Next, add in the onion and garlic. Allow it to cook for 1 minute, then add in the green beans, water, salt, and pepper.

Cook uncovered approximately 12–15 minutes until water has evaporated and beans are tender, stirring occasionally. If water has evaporated and beans are not tender, add in an additional ¼ cup of water and continue to cook until beans are tender.

MAKES 4 SERVINGS
Serving Size: ??
Calories: 106
Fat: 5g
Saturated fat: 2g
Polyunsaturated fat: 0g
Monounsaturated fat: 2g
Trans fat: 0g
Cholesterol: 11mg
Sodium: 539mg
Carbohydrates: 11g
Fiber: 2.5g
Sugar: 3g
Protein: 6g
Iron: 9g
Potassium: 297mg

Spinach Artichoke Pasta Bake

12 ounces rigatoni (measure dry)
1 tablespoon olive oil
1 large white onion, minced
½ teaspoon salt
½ teaspoon black pepper
4 cloves garlic, finely chopped
¾ cup sour cream
4 ounces cream cheese, softened to room temperature
½ cup parmesan cheese, grated
2 teaspoons fresh lemon zest
10 ounces frozen spinach, thawed and squeezed of moisture
14 ounces artichoke hearts in water, drained and chopped
1 ½ cup mozzarella cheese, shredded

Boil pasta until tender according to instructions on package. Reserve ½ cup of the pasta water and drain the rest.

In a large skillet over medium heat, heat the olive oil. Add in the onion, salt, and pepper. Cover and stir occasionally until tender (about 8 minutes). Add in the garlic and cook while stirring for 1 minute.

Turn your oven broiler on. In a large bowl, combine the sour cream, cream cheese, parmesan, lemon zest, and lemon juice. Stir into the onion mixture.

Add the cooked pasta to the bowl and stir gently to coat. Then stir in the spinach, artichokes, and ¼ cup of the reserved water from the pasta. Add a little more at a time if pasta seems dry. Next, fold in ½ cup mozzarella.

Spoon the pasta into an oven-safe 3-quart casserole dish. Sprinkle the top with remaining mozzarella and broil until golden brown, around 5 minutes.

MAKES 8 SERVINGS
Serving size: 1 cup
Calories: 358
Fat: 6g
Saturated fat: 8g
Polyunsaturated fat: 0g
Monounsaturated fat: 2.5g
Trans fat: 0g
Cholesterol: 37mg
Sodium: 450mg
Carbohydrates: 38g
Fiber: 2g
Sugar: 3g
Protein: 17g
Iron: 10g
Potassium: 99mg

Grandma's Buttermilk Fried Chicken

1 cup all-purpose flour
½ cup cornstarch
1 tablespoon + 1 teaspoon of sea salt (more to taste)
1 teaspoon of pepper, divided (more to taste)
½ quart buttermilk
2 pounds bone-in chicken of choice
2 cups vegetable oil for frying

In a shallow, wide dish, whisk flour, cornstarch, 1 teaspoon salt, and ½ teaspoon pepper. Once well mixed, set aside.

In a large bowl, whisk together buttermilk, 1 tablespoon salt, and ½ teaspoon pepper. Dip chicken into flour mixture and then submerge chicken into buttermilk mix. Cover and place in the fridge for 3–8 hours. Cover flour mixture and reserve for frying.

When ready to fry, heat oil in a cast-iron skillet over medium heat until oil reaches 350°.

One piece at a time, remove chicken from buttermilk, letting excess drip off. Then coat chicken in flour mixture. Careful to avoid splashing, place chicken into hot oil. Fry for 16–20 minutes* and flip one time halfway through. Remove chicken and place onto a paper towel-lined dish or pan to absorb excess oil.

*If frying boneless chicken pieces, fry time will be approximately 7–10 minutes or until juices run clear.

MAKES 8 SERVINGS
Serving size: 1 piece
Calories: 588
Fat: 45g
Saturated fat: 9g
Polyunsaturated fat: 16g
Monounsaturated fat: 6g
Trans fat: 0g
Protein: 25g
Carbohydrates: 22g
Fiber: 0g
Sugar: 4g
Cholesterol: 103mg
Sodium: 1135mg
Iron: 11g
Potassium: 4mg

Candy Apply Trifle

2 8-ounce packages of cream cheese, softened
1 tablespoon vanilla extract
2 cups powdered sugar
16 ounces Cool Whip
5 Granny Smith apples, cored and cubed into bite-sized pieces
7 Snickers bars, chopped
1 jar ice cream topping caramel sauce
4 tablespoons chopped peanuts

In a large mixing bowl, beat the cream cheese until smooth using a hand mixer. Using a low speed, add the vanilla extract and add in the powdered sugar ½ cup at a time. When well mixed, fold in the Cool Whip. Stir in the chopped apples, leaving a few out to use on the top as garnish. Stir in 1 cup of the chopped Snickers.

Spoon ⅓ of the mixture into the bottom of a trifle bowl or clear glass serving dish. Sprinkle with a few more of the Snickers pieces around the edges and drizzle entire layer with caramel sauce. Continue to layer into 2–3 layers, depending upon the size of your dish. Top with the remaining Snickers and apples for garnish, drizzle with remaining caramel sauce, and sprinkle with chopped peanuts.

Place in the fridge for 2 hours to chill or until ready to serve. I recommend serving it the same day you make it for the best flavor and presentation.

MAKES 15 SERVINGS
Serving size: ¾ cup
Calories: 414
Fat: 18g
Saturated fat: 10g
Polyunsaturated fat: 0g
Monounsaturated fat: 0g
Trans fat: 0g
Protein: 4.5g
Carbohydrates: 61g
Fiber: 2g
Sugar: 51g
Cholesterol: 38mg
Sodium: 240mg
Iron: 2g
Potassium: 8mg

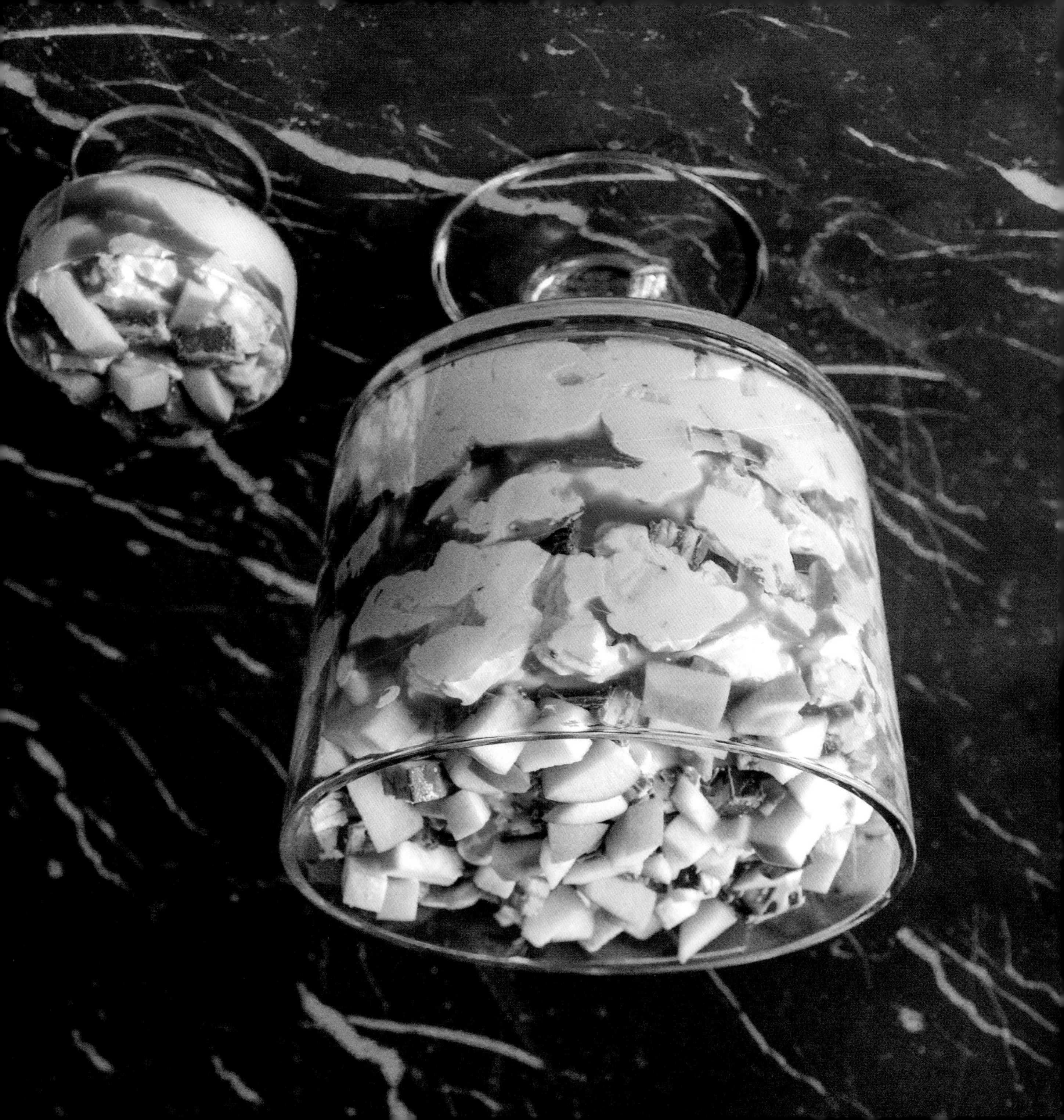

4 cups low-fat mozzarella cheese shreds

Using a 9-by-13-inch baking pan, layer noodles, spooning just enough egg mixture on top of noodles to apply a thin coat. Sprinkle with mozzarella, top with the meat sauce, and repeat. Finally, top with mozzarella, ensuring edges are covered with cheese to prevent the noodles from drying.

Bake for 30 minutes. Allow lasagna to rest 5 minutes before serving.

MAKES 12 SERVINGS

Serving size: 1 slice
Calories: 438
Fat: 17g
Saturated fat: 8.5g
Polyunsaturated fat: 0g
Monounsaturated fat: 0g
Trans fat: 0g
Protein: 29.5g
Carbohydrates: 44.5g
Fiber: 4g
Sugar: 5g
Cholesterol: 89mg
Sodium: 856mg
Iron: 24g
Potassium: 407mg

Chocolate Fluff Brownies

2 sticks of butter
3 cups semisweet chocolate chips
1 cup white sugar
1 cup light brown sugar, packed
1 teaspoon sea salt
2 eggs
1½ cups flour
2 cups mini marshmallows

Line a 9-by-13-inch baking pan with parchment paper and butter the paper on bottom and sides. Leave enough paper so that there is an overhang, so you can lift the brownies out.

In a double boiler or heat-safe bowl set over a saucepan of simmering water, combine butter and 2 cups of the chocolate chips. Heat and stir occasionally, just until melted.

Remove from heat and stir in white sugar, brown sugar, salt, eggs, and finally flour, until just combined. Spread batter evenly in prepared pan. Bake until toothpick comes out clean when inserted in the center, 35–40 minutes.

Remove brownies from the oven and sprinkle top with remaining chocolate chips and marshmallows. Bake for 5 minutes or until chocolate melts and marshmallows are puffed and start to brown.

Remove from oven and let cool 10 minutes, then lift brownies out by parchment paper and place onto a cooling rack. Cool completely before slicing.

MAKES 24 BROWNIES.
Serving size: 1 brownie
Calories: 320
Fat: 16g
Saturated fat: 10g
Polyunsaturated fat: 0g
Monounsaturated fat: 2g
Trans fat: 0g
Cholesterol: 35mg
Sodium: 149mg
Carbohydrates: 43g
Fiber: 0g
Sugar: 35g
Protein: 2.5g
Iron: 0.5g
Potassium: 20mg

Death by Chocolate Clusters

- **1 pound white chocolate almond bark, broken into pieces**
- **½ pound dark chocolate almond bark, broken into pieces**
- **2 ounces German chocolate bar**
- **6 ounces semisweet chocolate chips**
- **16 ounces lightly salted dry-roasted peanuts**
- **8 ounces whole almonds**
- **½ teaspoon almond extract**

Using a slow cooker, turn on high and add all chocolate and nuts (everything except the almond extract).

Cook for 45 minutes. Don't raise lid or stir.

Reduce heat to low setting and cook for 1 hour, stirring until all chocolate is melted. Add almond extract and stir well.

Using a tablespoon, spoon into mini muffin liners. Allow to set on countertop or in fridge. Once set, place in an airtight container.

MAKES 75 SERVINGS
Serving size: 1 piece
Calories: 114
Fat: 8g
Saturated fat: 3g
Polyunsaturated fat: 1g
Monounsaturated fat: 2g
Trans fat: 0g
Cholesterol: 1mg
Sodium: 39mg
Carbohydrates: 8g
Fiber: 1g
Sugar: 5g
Protein: 3g
Iron: 4g
Potassium: 66mg

Peanut Butter Cheese Ball

8 ounces cream cheese, softened to room temperature
1 cup powdered sugar
¾ cup creamy peanut butter
3 tablespoons packed brown sugar
¾ cup milk chocolate chips
¾ cup peanut butter chips
graham crackers, apple slices, or vanilla wafers for dipping

Using a hand mixer and a medium mixing bowl, beat together cream cheese, powdered sugar, peanut butter, and brown sugar.

Spoon into a large piece of plastic wrap. Bring up all 4 corners and twist tightly to form a ball. (Alternatively, you may make 2 smaller balls, dividing mix onto 2 pieces of plastic wrap.)

Freeze for an hour and a half or until the cheese ball is firm enough to keep its shape. Place the chocolate chips and peanut butter chips on a plate. Remove the plastic wrap and roll the ball, pressing the chips lightly to cover the ball completely.

Place the ball on a serving dish, cover, and freeze for 2 hours or until almost firm. Alternatively, you can freeze overnight and allow it to thaw at room temperature for 20 minutes before serving.

Spread onto your favorite crackers, cookies, or fruit slices!

MAKES 12 SERVINGS
Serving size: ¼ cup
Calories: 373
Fat: 22.5g
Saturated fat: 11.5g
Polyunsaturated fat: 0g
Monounsaturated fat: 0g
Trans fat: 0g
Cholesterol: 23 mg
Sodium: 176mg
Carbohydrates: 35g
Fiber: 2g
Sugar: 29g
Protein: 9g
Iron: 9g
Potassium: 5mg

Coconut Cream Dreams

½ cup butter
2 cups powdered sugar, sifted
3 cups flaked coconut
36 pieces of milk chocolate chips

Melt butter in a medium saucepan. Remove from heat. Add sugar and coconut and mix well.

Shape into rounded teaspoons or use a small cookie scoop, then place onto a cookie sheet lined with wax paper. Make a small indention in the top of each cookie, then place a chocolate chip in the center of each.

Place in the fridge and allow them to chill until firm. Then store in an airtight container in the fridge.

MAKES 3 DOZEN COOKIES
Serving size: 1 cookie
Calories: 95
Fat: 5.5g
Saturated fat: 4g
Polyunsaturated fat: 0g
Monounsaturated fat: 0g
Trans fat: 0g
Cholesterol: 6.5mg
Sodium: 38mg
Carbohydrates: 10.5g
Fiber: 1.4g
Sugar: 9g
Protein: 0g
Iron: 0g
Potassium: 0.5mg

Nighty-Night Cookies

2 egg whites*
⅔ cup white sugar*
1 cup chopped pecans or walnuts
1 cup chocolate chips

Preheat oven to 350°.

Using a hand mixer, beat egg whites until stiff white peaks form. (It will look like Cool Whip when it's ready.)

Gradually add in sugar and continue to beat. Then fold in nuts and chocolate chips.

Drop by the teaspoon onto foil-lined cookie sheet.

Put in the oven and turn oven off. Do not open until the morning.

*Don't use liquid egg whites or a sugar substitute.

MAKES 3 DOZEN COOKIES
Serving size: 1 cookie
Calories: 66
Fat: 4g
Saturated fat: 1g
Polyunsaturated fat: 0.5g
Monounsaturated fat: 1g
Trans fat: 0g
Cholesterol: 0mg
Sodium: 3mg
Carbohydrates: 8g
Fiber: 0.5g
Sugar: 7g
Protein: 0.5g
Iron: 0g
Potassium: 15mg

Praline Pecan Crunch

8 cups Quaker Oatmeal Squares
2 cups pecan pieces
½ cup light corn syrup
½ cup firmly packed brown sugar
¼ cup butter
1 teaspoon vanilla extract
½ teaspoon baking soda

Preheat oven to 250°.

In a 9-by-13-inch baking pan, combine cereal and pecans. Set aside.

In a microwave-safe, medium-sized bowl, combine corn syrup, brown sugar, and butter. Microwave 90 seconds and stir. Microwave again for 30–90 seconds, until boiling. Remove from microwave using pot holders.

Stir in vanilla and baking soda, then pour over cereal mixture. Stir to coat evenly.

Bake 1 hour, stirring every 20 minutes.

Spread on baking sheet to cool, then break into pieces.

MAKES 20 SERVINGS
Serving size: ½ cup
Calories: 224
Fat: 11g
Saturated fat: 2g
Polyunsaturated fat: 2.5g
Monounsaturated fat: 4.5g
Trans fat: 0g
Cholesterol: 0mg
Sodium: 112mg
Carbohydrates: 33g
Fiber: 3g
Sugar: 16g
Protein: 3.5g
Iron: 37g
Potassium: 132mg

Blueberry Crumble Muffins

FOR MUFFINS

- nonstick cooking spray or muffin tin liners
- 1 ½ cups all-purpose flour
- ¾ cup white sugar, divided
- ½ teaspoon salt
- 2 teaspoons baking powder
- ⅓ cup vegetable oil
- 1 egg
- ⅓ cup 2% milk
- 1 ½ cups fresh blueberries

FOR CRUMBLE TOPPING

- ½ cup white sugar
- ⅓ cup all-purpose flour
- ¼ cup butter, cubed
- 1 ½ teaspoons ground cinnamon

Preheat oven to 400°.

Line muffin tin with liners or spray with nonstick cooking spray.

In a medium mixing bowl, combine 1½ cups flour, ¾ cup sugar, salt, and baking powder. Place vegetable oil in a 1-cup measuring cup, then add the egg and just enough milk to fill to the top of the cup. Mix this in with the flour mixture, then gently fold in the blueberries. Fill muffin cups to the top.

In a small bowl, add crumble topping ingredients and mix with a fork until crumbly and fluffy. Then sprinkle topping over the muffins.

Bake for 18–22 minutes or until a toothpick inserted in the muffin comes out clean.

MAKES 8 SERVINGS
Serving size: 1 muffin
Calories: 372
Fat: 16g
Saturated fat: 5g
Polyunsaturated fat: 6.5g
Monounsaturated fat: 2g
Trans fat: 0g
Cholesterol: 24mg
Sodium: 139mg
Carbohydrates: 56g
Fiber: 4g
Sugar: 34g
Protein: 5g
Iron: 6.5g
Potassium: 166mg

1 teaspoon garlic salt
¾ teaspoon sea salt
2 tablespoons butter
2 tablespoons Crisco
1 cup mild cheddar cheese, shredded
1 cup cold buttermilk
2 tablespoons fresh chives, minced

salt, and sea salt.

Mix butter and Crisco into the flour mixture with your hands until dough is crumbly. Make a well in the middle of the dough and pour in cheese, buttermilk, and chives. Mix with your hands until incorporated. Do not use a hand mixer, as it will overwork the dough.

Flour a clean work surface and place the dough on it. Sprinkle extra flour on top to make it easier to work with. Gently roll out the dough, and then fold dough in half six times, gently rolling each time to form layers. Roll out to 1 inch thick and cut out biscuits using a 2–3 inch round biscuit or cookie cutter.

Place cut biscuits onto an ungreased baking sheet with biscuits touching but not pressed against each other.

Combine scraps, rolling out the dough and folding it over 4 times, then cut remaining biscuits. Discard any scraps at that point; you only want to take 2 cuttings.

Bake for 15–20 minutes until they are a light golden brown on top.

MAKES 14 SERVINGS
Serving size: 1 biscuit
Calories: 129
Fat: 7g
Saturated fat: 3g
Polyunsaturated fat: 1g
Monounsaturated fat: 1g
Trans fat: 0g
Cholesterol: 9.5mg
Sodium: 296mg
Carbohydrates: 14.5g
Fiber: 2g
Sugar: 1g
Protein: 5g
Iron: 3.5g
Potassium: 69mg

3 cups oil
2 cups cornmeal
1 cup flour
2 cloves garlic, minced
¼ cup diced jalapeños
1 tablespoon white sugar
1 ½ teaspoons baking powder
1 teaspoon salt
½ teaspoon baking soda
½ teaspoon black pepper
2 cups buttermilk
1 egg
½ cup shredded cheddar cheese

Heat oil in stockpot over medium heat until it reaches and stays at 350°. You may need more or less oil depending on the size of your stockpot.

In a large mixing bowl, mix together cornmeal, flour, garlic, jalapeños, sugar, baking powder, salt, baking soda, and pepper.

In a small bowl, mix together the buttermilk and egg. Stir buttermilk mixture into the dry ingredients. Once mixed, stir in cheddar cheese.

Working in small batches, scoop batter by the tablespoon or with a medium-sized cookie scoop. Drop the scoops of batter into the oil and fry for 8–10 minutes, or until golden brown. Remove and place on a baking sheet lined with a paper towel to allow excess oil to drip off. Serve warm.

MAKES 12 SERVINGS

Serving size: 2 hush puppies
Calories: 130
Fat: 5g
Saturated fat: 1g
Polyunsaturated fat: 2g
Monounsaturated fat: 0.5g
Trans fat: 0g
Cholesterol: 14mg
Sodium: 93mg
Carbohydrates: 19g
Fiber: 1g
Sugar: 2g
Protein: 4g
Iron: 2g
Potassium: 30mg

Cook the beef in a pan, drain the juices, and season with salt and pepper.

Spray the bottom and edges of a slow cooker with cooking spray for easy clean-up.

Place Velveeta and beef in slow cooker and set on low. Stir occasionally, until Velveeta is melted and smooth.

Next, add in black beans, Ro-Tel, and jalapeños. Stir until combined. Add salsa to help thin mixture. Keep slow cooker on low or a warm setting and stir occasionally. Serve warm.

MAKES 12 SERVINGS

Serving size: ¾ cup
Calories: 311
Fat: 14g
Saturated fat: 6g
Polyunsaturated fat: 0g
Monounsaturated fat: 0g
Trans fat: 0g
Cholesterol: 65mg
Sodium: 1,374mg
Carbohydrates: 22g
Fiber: 6g
Sugar: 7g
Protein: 24g
Iron: 6g
Potassium: 334mg

Spinach and Artichoke Dip

- **9–11 ounces frozen creamed spinach, thawed**
- **1 6-ounce jar marinated artichoke hearts, drained and chopped roughly**
- **¼ cup full-fat mayonnaise**
- **¼ cup full-fat sour cream**
- **1 garlic clove, pressed**
- **½ cup grated parmesan cheese**
- **¼ cup mozzarella cheese, shredded (optional)**
- **Tortilla chips, pita chips, or toasted bread**

Preheat oven to 375°.

In a medium bowl, combine creamed spinach, artichokes, mayonnaise, and sour cream. Mix until well combined.

Stir in pressed garlic and parmesan cheese. Pour mixture into a baking dish. Optionally, top with mozzarella cheese shreds.

Bake for 20–25 minutes, until dip is heated through and the mozzarella on top is melted. Serve with tortilla chips, pita chips, toasted bread, or whatever you prefer to dip!

MAKES 6 SERVINGS
Serving size: ⅓ cup
Calories: 152
Fat: 13g
Saturated fat: 5g
Polyunsaturated fat: 5g
Monounsaturated fat: 3g
Trans fat: 0g
Cholesterol: 22mg
Sodium: 677mg
Carbohydrates: 5g
Fiber: 2g
Sugar: 2g
Protein: 5g
Iron: 3g
Potassium: 24mg

Beer-Battered French Fries

1 cup flour
1 teaspoon garlic salt
1 teaspoon onion salt
1 teaspoon sea salt
2 teaspoons black pepper
1 teaspoon paprika
½ cup of your favorite beer
2 ½ pounds russet potatoes, peeled
2 cups oil (more or less depending upon your skillet size)

Heat oil over medium-high heat.

Mix flour, garlic salt, onion salt, sea salt, black pepper, and paprika in a medium bowl. Add beer and whisk to combine. (You may need more or less beer. Add beer until you achieve a consistency you could drizzle.)

Cut potatoes into fries. Dip individually in beer batter, and then place in oil. Do not let them touch at first or they will stick together. Let fry until golden brown.

Remove and place on a paper towel-lined plate to absorb excess oil. Sprinkle with additional salt and pepper and serve immediately.

MAKES 6 SERVINGS
Serving size: 6 ounces
Calories: 428
Fat: 14g
Saturated fat: 1g
Polyunsaturated fat: 4g
Monounsaturated fat: 8g
Trans fat: 0g
Cholesterol: 0mg
Sodium: 840mg
Carbohydrates: 70g
Fiber: 6g
Sugar: 2g
Protein: 9g
Iron: 17g
Potassium: 1451mg

In a small, microwave-safe bowl, heat the butter and honey until melted and smooth, then stir in green onions and drizzle over the potato wedges evenly. Enjoy!

MAKES 4 SERVINGS

4 wedges per serving

Calories: 495

Fat: 43g

Saturated fat: 12g

Polyunsaturated fat: 8g

Monounsaturated fat: 19g

Trans fat: 0g

Cholesterol: 53mg

Sodium: 567mg

Carbohydrates: 23g

Fiber: 1g

Sugar: 10g

Protein: 9g

Iron: 7g

Potassium: 438mg

pie crusts.

Place pie plate on baking sheet just in case the filling bubbles over. Place the pie in oven and bake for 30–35 minutes or until pie crust is golden brown and filling is bubbly.

Remove from oven and allow to cool 10 minutes before serving. Cut into 6 even slices.

MAKES 6 SERVINGS

Serving size: 1/6 of pie

Calories: 488

Fat: 28g

Saturated fat: 13g

Polyunsaturated fat: 1g

Monounsaturated fat: 9g

Trans fat: 0g

Cholesterol: 46mg

Sodium: 659mg

Carbohydrates: 40g

Fiber: 2g

Sugar: 4g

Protein: 17g

Iron: 3g

Potassium: 194mg

½ teaspoon salt
1 garlic clove, minced
pinch of pepper
⅓ cup parmesan cheese
cup chopped green onions

Add milk, butter, parsley, salt, and garlic together in a pan. Heat on medium-high until butter melts, stirring often. Reduce heat, stirring occasionally until sauce thickens.

Combine bacon, broccoli, and mushrooms, hot cavatelli, milk mixture, and parmesan cheese. Toss to coat.

Garnish with green onions and serve immediately.

*Cheat sheet: You may use a jar of ready-made alfredo sauce instead of homemade sauce to save a little time if you're in a pinch.

MAKES 6 SERVINGS
Serving size: 1.5 cups
Calories: 392
Fat: 21g
Saturated fat: 12g
Polyunsaturated fat: 1g
Monounsaturated fat: 6g
Trans fat: 0g
Cholesterol: 53mg
Sodium: 780mg
Carbohydrates: 34g
Fiber: 3g
Sugar: 5g
Protein: 19g
Iron: 11g
Potassium: 206mg

Italian Garlic Parmesan Chicken

- 1 package of Good Seasons brand dry Italian dressing mix
- ½ teaspoon of garlic
- ¾ cup grated parmesan cheese
- 1 egg, beaten
- 4 boneless, skinless chicken breasts, pounded out evenly

Preheat oven to 425° and line a baking sheet with parchment paper.

In a small bowl, combine dry Italian dressing mix, garlic, and parmesan cheese. In another bowl, place the beaten egg.

Dip the chicken in the egg, allowing excess to drip off. Then place chicken into the dry mixture and pat gently to coat both sides. Place on baking sheet and repeat with all chicken breasts.

Place in oven and bake for 20–25 minutes or until internal temperature reaches 165°.

MAKES 4 SERVINGS

Serving size: 6 ounces
Calories: 445
Fat: 24g
Saturated fat: 13g
Polyunsaturated fat: 0g
Monounsaturated fat: 7g
Trans fat: 0g
Cholesterol: 100mg
Sodium: 1929mg
Carbohydrates: 3g
Fiber: 0g
Sugar: 0g
Protein: 49g
Iron: 5g
Potassium: 90mg

I was beyond excited to write this cookbook and have all my healthy favorites and some of my most favorite indulgences in one book. The recipes you'll find on this side of the book are recipes I created and also acquired through the years from my family and friends. This side serves almost as a testament to all the memories I have from my childhood into adult life.

If you think about it, social events revolve around great food, which brings even better memories. These are the recipes that are flavorful memories for me. Sunday dinners with crispy fried chicken. My mom's lasagna—still a favorite to this day. Blueberry muffins with a flaky crumb topping for breakfast after camping. Fresh-from-the-fryer hush puppies. These are all enjoyed in moderation. Health is about balance.

Balance is eating healthy 80 percent of the time while having some of our most beloved comfort foods, like the ones in this way to achieve the healthy balance you crave all in one place.

–Emily Frisella

Contents

THE Sinner's Dinner

BY EMILY FRISELLA